Trade-Off

Trade-Off

Why Some Things Catch On,
and Others Don't

Kevin Maney

Broadway Books

NEW YORK

Copyright © 2009 by Kevin Maney

Published in the United States by Broadway Books, an imprint of the Crown Publishing Group, a division of Random House, Inc., New York.
www.crownpublishing.com

BROADWAY BOOKS and the Broadway Books colophon are trademarks of Random House, Inc.

Library of Congress Cataloging-in-Publication Data
Maney, Kevin, 1960–
Trade-off : why some things catch on, and others don't / Kevin Maney.—1st ed.
1. Technological innovations—Economic aspects—History. I. Title.
HC79.T4M3474 2009
338'.064—dc22   2009023318

ISBN 978-0-385-52594-7

Printed in the United States of America

10 9 8 7 6 5 4 3 2 1

First Edition

For my mom, who has shown me a thing or two about strength.

CONTENTS

PART THREE /
THE TRADE-OFF IN PRACTICE

ACKNOWLEDGMENTS

I'm not a great believer in fate, but sometimes the universe conspires in beguiling ways—and when it does, you have to go with it.

Many things in my work life were pointing to this book. But then, after I put a proposal together and my terrific agent, Sandy Dijkstra, floated it to editors, I ran smack into the worst personal crisis in my adult life. Just when I desperately needed some good news, Sandy called on a Monday to say that Roger Scholl at Doubleday was enthusiastic about the idea. By Thursday we had a deal. Everything seemed to come together at just the right moment, and you're holding the result.

So, thank you, Roger and Sandy, for believing in this idea and helping to see it through.

I want to thank some of the smartest people I know for helping me work out the concepts. Ted Leonsis met me at his office at the Washington Capitals practice rink. Marc Andreessen drew graphs in my notebook at his favorite restaurant, Hobee's, in Palo Alto, California. Jeff Bezos talked with me in a conference room at Condé Nast in New York. Kodak's executive team pounded on my fidelity-swap ideas on an unusually warm February afternoon in Rochester, New York. And here in Virginia's Fairfax County, George Mason University business professor J. P. Auffret helped me over the course of many lunches.

Thanks, also, to *Condé Nast Portfolio* magazine, which I joined in 2007. Unfortunately, it died in April 2009 as I was finishing this book. My editors there were supportive of this project. And I want to acknowledge *USA Today*, where I spent almost half my life and learned most of what I know about journalism. Scattered portions of this book first appeared in *Portfolio* or *USA Today*.

A thank-you goes out to my brother Scott. His advertising and design firm, Jones Inc., created the fidelity-swap graphic.

Finally, thanks to Alison and Sam. I'd always been told that kids turn into aliens when they hit their teenage years. They've proved the conventional wisdom wrong, and I've never enjoyed them more than while seeing them through high school and everything that's gone with it. Here's to hoping this book helps pay for college.

FOREWORD

By Jim Collins

In 1992, I had my first of many conversations with Kevin Maney. Kevin, then a young technology reporter for *USA Today,* called me at my office at the Stanford Graduate School of Business to discuss the life cycles of entrepreneurial companies. Kevin had been working on a story about Apple, and he was trying to make sense of the company's erratic trajectory. I returned Kevin's call, and we had an hour-long conversation that began with me pummeling him with questions. What did he see as the challenges for Apple? Why did he think that Apple had underestimated Microsoft? What did he think of Apple trying to make itself into a business computing company? What did he make of the Newton? Kevin impressed me with his prescient view that the passing of time would show Apple's ouster of Steve Jobs in the mid-1980s to be one of the most colossal blunders in American business history. Keep in mind: this was 1992, with Jobs off in the wilderness, fully five years before Jobs's triumphant return to Apple.

Kevin Maney stood out to me then—and stands out to me today—as one of the most insightful journalists about the dynamic world of technology, the companies that rise and fall based on those technologies, and the people who seek to change the world through those technologies. Kevin has a peculiar genius for seeing what makes people tick. And it is, after all, *people* who invent new technologies, build companies, destroy companies, exercise power, act with wisdom, and engage in folly. Whether it be conversations with sages like Andy Grove, transformational leaders like Anne Mulcahy, creative entrepreneurs like Bill Gates, or societal figures like Michael Bloomberg, Kevin brings a sort of Vulcan-mind-meld ability to his work; he listens and observes with precision, makes sense of what he has heard, and then finds a way to communicate it to the rest of us with great clarity.

In the two decades he worked as technology columnist for *USA Today,* he wrote more than six hundred columns, plus dozens of feature stories and two books. He held a front-row seat for some of the most significant technology and business stories, sitting right smack in the middle of the boom and bust cycles of the 1990s and 2000s. He covered the rise of the Internet, the Netscape supernova and subsequent browser wars, the near-death and resurrection of Apple, the vise grip on the personal computer industry enjoyed by Microsoft, the loosening of that vise grip in recent years, the near-destruction of IBM and its spectacular resurrection, the Googlizing of the world, the creation of AOL and the ill-starred Time Warner deal, the rise and fall and near-collapse of Motorola, the birth of a capitalist computer industry in Russia, the early Internet in China, and dozens of other major stories. Throughout, he interviewed key protagonists and extracted meaning from the melee; he not only covered the rapid evolution of technologies, companies, and industries, but—most important—he *made sense* of them *as* they evolved.

Along the way, he came to a conclusion about the best

people he'd covered: They have the courage to make rigorous choices. They don't delude themselves into thinking they can do everything, so they focus on only what they can do with great distinction.

His conclusion rings true. Without question, the best leaders we've studied across our research into what makes great companies displayed tremendous discipline in their decisions. They did not succumb to undisciplined pursuit of growth and short-term success. They did not sway with the political wind—this way and that—and they adhered fanatically to a set of core values. They paid tremendous attention not just to what to do, but equally to what *not* to do.

Building on this idea, Kevin now stands back in this book to synthesize all of his work into a single concept that helps to explain and integrate much of what he's observed. His concept: that those who have the courage to make rigorous choices between high-fidelity and high-convenience do better than those who make no clear and rigorous choices. A strategic lens—such as the one provided here in *Trade-Off*—does not in itself give an answer about what you should do, and not do. Rather—and much better—it forces you to engage in a powerful question, from which you derive your own insight and make your own decisions. If you engage your team in a vigorous debate stimulated by the questions that naturally arise from the ideas in these pages, you will gain deeper understanding not just of what you should be doing (or not) but, even more important, *why*. The power of a strategic concept lies first and foremost in giving us a lens and a stimulus for hard thinking and hard choices. The critical question is not its universal truth, but its usefulness. And in this, I believe Kevin Maney has extracted a very useful framework.

As Kevin was finishing up the manuscript for this book, I took him on a rock climb up the First Flatiron, a one-thousand-foot sandstone slab that looms above my home in Boulder, Colorado. Not a climber, Kevin found the experience exhilarating and exhausting ("I feel like I've been in a car wreck" he wrote the next day). After terrifying him for a few hours, we reached the top, and we began a leisurely amble toward home, full of animated conversation about this new book.

He launched into an impassioned discussion about the desperate need for disciplined trade-offs. If business leaders fail to make choices—fanatical, obsessive, focused, disciplined choices—to build for the long term, and succumb instead to grasping as much as they can in the short term, they will build mediocre companies. If political leaders fail to make hard choices—about what works, what doesn't, and what we can sustainably afford—they will propel their nations into historical mediocrity. If schools fail to focus on what delivers education results, if health-care systems fail to make choices that improve patient outcomes, if churches fail to distinguish between congregation growth and spiritual growth, if nonprofits succumb to mission creep, then we'll have mediocre social sectors and a mediocre society. If our young people fail to understand that they have to make choices and live with the consequences of those choices, they will become mediocre adults.

"So, I take it that your concept applies to individual people, their lives and careers?" I asked.

"Yes," he replied. "You've got to make trade-offs to become distinctive, rather than merely employable. You've got to find a way to turn yourself from just another person that can be hired, one of many that could do a given job."

We talked about how most people settle for a good life rather than a great life, because they fail to make the disciplined choices. Kevin remarked that he had referenced a good-to-great idea, the Hedgehog Concept, in his final chapter precisely to make this point. To have a personal Hedgehog Concept means that you have constructed a path that meets three tests (the intersection of three circles): 1) passion (you adhere to your core values and do what you love to do); 2) genetic encoding (you do what you are genetically encoded for, activities you are made to do exceptionally well); 3) valuable contribution (you engage in work that makes a contribution of economic and social value, that gives you an economic engine for life). Kevin's concept of fidelity (being something special and hard to get) versus convenience (being easily accessible, even at the expense of lower quality) means carving an idiosyncratic path that is uniquely tailored to you. Better to be valuable and unique than to be valuable and just like a bunch of other people.

And that's what Kevin Maney himself has done. Instead of defining himself as "columnist at *USA Today*" he has struck out on his own, to carve his own idiosyncratic path, defined by his own unique three circles. He has made the trade-off between a traditional path, defined by a traditional job, and the creative path, self-defined by his work. His job description: Kevin Maney. He is one of those rare people who has not only found his three circles, but has made the choices to live them.

Jim Collins
Boulder, Colorado
June 2009

Trade-Off

Introduction

In the fall of 2005, I sat in a cavernous San Francisco hotel ballroom at a tech conference called Web 2.0, all 3,000 of us in the audience jammed so tightly in narrow chairs that the joke went around that the event was being managed by Southwest Airlines. On stage were the CEO of Netflix, Reed Hastings, and Mark Cuban, the billionaire tech bad boy most famous for owning the Dallas Mavericks NBA team. I have little recollection of what the two of them said up there, except for the moment when Hastings talked about his philosophy for running Netflix. The company's business was built on renting out movies by mailing the DVDs to customers, who would mail them back after watching. Hastings felt he had to explain to the tech-savvy crowd why Netflix wasn't ready to change its reliance on something as old-fashioned as the Postal Service.

Most of Netflix's customers weren't willing to opt for the speed of an instant Internet download if it meant having to finagle with software and put up with the hassles of anti-piracy mechanisms. Getting a familiar disk by mail and dropping it into a DVD player made for a far easier, more satisfying experience.

Hastings said his strategic decisions at Netflix were driven by one simple core principle: People are willing to trade the quality of an experience for the convenience of getting it, and vice versa. In Hastings's estimation, getting DVDs by mail was a higher-quality experience at the time than speedy Internet downloads.

Over two decades of interviewing technology CEOs and entrepreneurs, I realized that dozens had told me some version of Hastings's principle, although they all had different phrases for it, and different ways of explaining the theory. When, a few years earlier, I'd interviewed Trip Hawkins, founder of the video game company Electronic Arts, about his new cell-phone gaming company called Digital Chocolate, he'd talked me through a similar philosophy. I'd had long conversations about this simple trade-off between quality and convenience with tech investor Roger McNamee in his office on Sand Hill Road in Menlo Park, California. Back in the early 1990s, Marc Porat, CEO of a much-hyped and ultimately doomed startup called General Magic, had rambled on about this same trade-off.

It occurred to me that Hastings's core concept was a terrific lens for viewing the way the world works. It can be an invaluable insight when dreaming up new products, when positioning brands, when planning company strategy, or when analyzing competitors. I couldn't get this simple yet powerful idea out of my head. So I talked with more people about it and refined the concept. In the summer of 2006, I shaped my research into a cover story for *USA Today,* and followed it up with a column that October. Both received an incredible response. In fact, none of the over 500 columns I had written in *USA Today* since the early 1990s had generated such a commotion. Significantly, the e-mails that came in weren't just from people in the tech industry.

I heard from the head of the Las Vegas W hotel—under construction at the time but since canceled—who wrote that he was going to send the column to his staff. I heard from the head of a strategy group for a major consulting company. I got e-mails from middle managers at midsized Midwestern companies. The column apparently struck a deep chord. And that response—that conversation with the business world—led me to write this book.

Kevin Maney
Centreville, Virginia,
2009

PART ONE

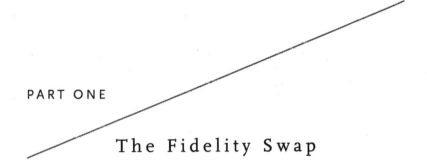

The Fidelity Swap

Prologue

The movie industry had a big problem. At its heart was the trade-off consumers were making between fidelity and convenience. So I went to see Hollywood's solution, and wound up on the set of *Avatar*.

Director James Cameron was shooting his 3-D movie in a building not much bigger than a high school gym. He wouldn't

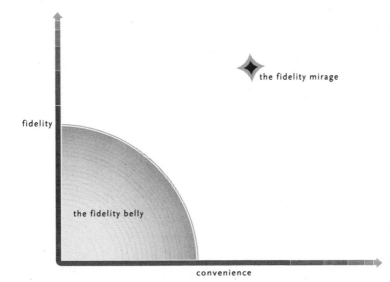

let anyone from the media inside—he is extraordinarily secretive about his shoots—so I waited to talk to Cameron's technology partner, Vince Pace, in a nearby unmarked building that served as the office for the shoot. The place could've been the headquarters of a Milwaukee ball-bearing wholesaler: wood veneer desks, fluorescent lights, thin beige carpeting. I was led into a conference room the size of a large walk-in closet. Pace finally arrived, wearing a blue golf shirt and jeans, carrying a paper plate loaded with barbecue and macaroni and cheese. It was lunch break on the *Avatar* set.

Pace developed the technology used to shoot almost every modern live-action 3-D movie—in some cases, co-developing it with Cameron. As he ate, Pace explained that the new 3-D technology was completely unlike 3-D from any other era. It's based on digital cinematography, which is relatively new to moviemaking. Pace invented dual-lens cameras that mimic the way a human's eyes capture an image from two slightly different angles. Computers digitize the images and allow a director to manipulate and edit them. That digital technology only became workable in the late 2000s, and it made shooting in 3-D a viable option—though it added as much as 20 percent to the cost of making a film.

"The tools and approaches are getting better and cheaper," Pace said. "This raises the bar for entertainment. I don't think 3-D can be stopped." Pace added that a 3-D movie like *Avatar* "is an experience people will want to pay for."

Hollywood is convinced Pace is right. DreamWorks co-founder Jeffrey Katzenberg pledged that all the studio's animated features would be made in 3-D. Cameron plans to make more 3-D movies after *Avatar.* Other superstar directors, including Peter Jackson *(Lord of the Rings)* and Robert Zemeckis *(Beowulf,*

A Christmas Carol) are making 3-D films. Every major studio is on board. Beginning in 2010, Hollywood will be releasing a parade of 3-D movies—all of this before a demonstrated long-term demand among the public for 3-D movies.

So, why leap into 3-D? Why the urgency?

In a sense, Hollywood studios latched onto 3-D for the same reason Bob Dole took Viagra. The essential part that drives Hollywood's business—theatrical showings—started going flaccid in the 2000s.

In the spring of 2008 the Motion Picture Association of America released numbers that, it claimed, showed that 2007 was a good year for the theatrical movie business. U.S. ticket revenue rose 5 percent, to $9.6 billion. But the 5-percent jump in revenue was entirely due to price increases. The number of tickets sold in the United States stayed flat from 2006 to 2007, at 1.4 billion. Worse, attendance was down from 2002, when it hit 1.6 billion. (In 1950, before TV took off, U.S. theaters annually sold 3 *billion* tickets.) The number of U.S. movie screens has been rising by 500 or more a year. In other words, theaters are seeing attendance per screen significantly diminish. Movies are doing worse than ever in theaters.

It is enough to give studio executives the vapors. Publicity and excitement from a theatrical release drives lucrative DVD sales and HBO showings, not to mention such ancillary moneymakers as toys and video games. "We make films for the theater and want to exhibit there first," Chuck Viane, president of distribution for Walt Disney, told me. "It's the engine that pulls the train."

Not knowing what else to do, Hollywood turned to 3-D, hoping to give people a cinema experience they couldn't get at home, and turn the theatrical movie business around. The problem for theaters is centered on the trade-off consumers make between the fidelity, or quality, of an experience and the convenience of getting it. Theaters of late have been sinking into a kind of consumer no-man's-land, what I call the *fidelity belly*—a place where neither the fidelity nor the convenience is good enough to attract a mass-market audience. Today the fidelity of watching a movie in a theater isn't hugely greater than the experience of watching a DVD on a large, flat-screen, high-definition TV at home. And home viewing comes with built-in advantages. You don't have a stranger in the seat next to you, and you can stop the movie to run to the bathroom, or get something to eat. On top of that, the convenience of a movie theater is not particularly good. You have to drive to the theater, pay a premium to see a film, and catch the movie at a set time that might not fit your schedule. Theaters can't make themselves much more convenient. The only way they can compete, apart from showing a movie before it's on DVD or cable, is by raising the fidelity of the movie theater experience. Hollywood believes 3-D can do that.

But the quality/convenience model teases out additional insights the industry seems to be overlooking. Three-D may be only a partial answer—or maybe even the wrong answer. If theaters try to simply out-fidelity home systems, they'll wind up in a constant arms race against home technology. Instead, theaters will have to offer an overall experience that's *different* from home viewing, and one that doesn't necessarily compete against home theaters. "We need to give people something they can't get at home," says Mike Thomson, vice president of operations for the Malco theater chain, which operates 320 screens in the U.S. heartland. Malco is one of many theater chains trying out ways to boost the cinema experience, such as offering waiter service, and featuring couches instead of traditional seats. "Three-D is a piece of the puzzle—but it's not the magic bullet," Thomson concludes.

Back on the *Avatar* set, Pace had to break off the conversation when he was needed to help Cameron set up a shot. Before he left, he talked about his business, which is called Pace. He believes it can expand dramatically and help studios make many of their movies in 3-D. He's an affable guy who has clearly invented valuable technology. But 3-D movies might not bring many more people through theater turnstiles. It's all about the trade-off consumers will make, and 3-D may not offer enough fidelity to offset the inconvenience of going out to a movie.

/ / /

Hollywood is by no means the only industry confronted with fidelity-convenience trade-offs. What I call the fidelity swap applies to almost any kind of business. It helps to explain the success of Steve Wynn's mega-hotels in Las Vegas, the impact of $2,500 economy cars introduced in 2008 by the Indian company Tata, and the reason the National Hockey League can't win a big American TV audience. It sheds light on newspapers' troubles in the mid-2000s, IBM's support for the Linux operating system, and the rise of text messaging among teens. The fidelity swap is not a new phenomenon. One can find that it explains the success of a patent medicine called Swamp Root in the 1870s, the breakthrough in 1900 of Eastman Kodak's first Brownie camera, and Clarence Birdseye's development of the frozen food business in 1924.

This profound trade-off gives businesspeople a new framework for talking and arguing about strategy and products and services. Knowing how the trade-off works can help CEOs figure out which R&D projects to green-light. It can help marketers determine how to position existing products, and give management a way to think through approaches to fix a business that's broken.

The fidelity swap is born of interviews with dozens of companies. Kodak vice president Betty Noonan noted that the model is "a moving, breathing decision tool—that's what I like about it." The fidelity swap challenges classic business-school teaching that tells you to make a chart on an x and y axis—and try to push your business into the upper right quadrant of the chart. In fact, in this model, gunning for the coveted upper right quadrant, where a company tries to achieve both high fidelity and high convenience, can bring a company crashing down—exactly what happened to Starbucks in 2007 and 2008.

Jeff Bezos, founder of Amazon.com, gave me the best description of the value of the fidelity swap. He and I spent an hour talking about this trade-off in New York in 2008, as we argued about where Amazon's e-book reader, the Kindle, fit in. Bezos said that the fidelity swap's real value is that it creates labels and a language to understand a business phenomenon that a lot of people instinctively already know, but can't quite articulate or express. The ensuing conversation will help companies and people work together to make better decisions.

That will be valuable in good times and bad. In the last stages of writing this book, the global economy dove into a recession. A difficult economy makes the fidelity swap even more vital, since companies have less room for mistakes. Yet in high-growth times, resources flow into new products and services, and the principles of the fidelity swap can help them succeed. The fidelity versus convenience trade-off happens in all economic conditions.

CHAPTER ONE

The Fidelity Swap

We constantly, in our everyday lives, make trade-offs between the fidelity of an experience and its convenience. It happens when we decide to watch a baseball game on TV instead of going to the park, make a phone call instead of meeting face-to-face, eat fast food at McDonald's instead of a nice meal at a restaurant, or buy $300 noise-canceling Bose headsets instead of using the inexpensive earbuds that come with the music player. Businesses, nonprofits, and governments make the same kinds of trade-offs in their buying decisions.

The way those trade-offs work and play out in the marketplace is the key to countless business successes and failures. This is the fidelity swap.

This fidelity swap has been going on since humans invented commerce. But the role of technology today accelerates the whole process.

There are five key concepts behind the fidelity swap:

Fidelity versus convenience. Fidelity is the total experience of something. At a rock concert, for instance, it's not just the quality of the sound—which often isn't as good as listening to a CD on a home stereo—but also everything else going on. That includes visually seeing the band, the lights and effects, the crowd around you, even the fact that you can later tell people you went to a particular concert and saw The Who, or Coldplay, live. It's all part of what makes up fidelity.

Convenience is how easy or hard it is to get what you want. That includes whether it's readily available, whether it's easy to do or use, and how much it costs. If something is less expensive, it's naturally more convenient because it's easier for more people to get it. In music, a downloaded song from iTunes is tremendously convenient—available anytime, easy to use, and inexpensive. It is, however, relatively low fidelity—a downloaded song file typically has ten times less audio information than the same song on a CD.

Consumers constantly trade fidelity for convenience, and vice versa. Once in a while you may go to an astoundingly inconvenient U2 concert simply because the fidelity of the experience cannot be replicated. Most of the time, however, we'll choose the low-fidelity, high-convenience experience: listening to U2 on a digital music player stuffed in a pocket.

But our fidelity-versus-convenience decisions are not static. They change with circumstance, sometimes moment to moment. And people with different priorities—those who have more, or less, discretionary income, those with more or less time on their hands, different age groups—make different trade-offs.

The tech effect. Technology constantly improves both fidelity and convenience. If a product or service is the highest fidelity today, technology and innovation will soon make it possible to create a product or service of higher fidelity. The same is true of convenience. These boundaries move over time. Nothing about the fidelity swap stays fixed.

The fidelity belly. Any product or service that is neither extremely high-fidelity nor high-convenience risks sinking into what I call the *fidelity belly*—the no-man's-land of consumer experience. It is a land ruled by apathy. No one gets very excited about a product or service that has so-so fidelity, and is only somewhat convenient. This is the problem movie theaters are falling into. It is the same problem hurting music CD sales. Because the tech effect keeps expanding the outer edges of fidelity and convenience, it expands or redefines the borders of the fidelity belly at the same time. The expanding belly swallows products and services that don't improve and keep pace with technology advancements.

The fidelity mirage. Contrary to what many businesses want to believe, achieving both high fidelity and high convenience seems to be impossible. It looks tempting. Some companies believe they can get there, and life will be beautiful. But as it turns out, any company or product that attempts to capture both is likely to fail, wasting resources and time. Starbucks and the luxury goods maker Coach are companies that have attempted this, only to crash to earth.

Super-fidelity or super-convenience. This defines the winners. Most successful products fall either at the far end of the fidelity axis or at the far end of the convenience axis. Apple landed the iPhone at the top of the fidelity axis in the cell-phone market, and it was an instant success despite its high price tag and limited availability. Wal-Mart won its leading-retailer position by becoming the high-convenience winner, making shopping for basics easier and cheaper than anywhere else. The fidelity of Wal-Mart is poor, just as the pricey iPhone started off as inconvenient. But that didn't matter. A way to win is to get to the top of one axis or the other.

Here are two significant additional factors to watch for:

Social accelerants. Our connection with others and our individual identity matter more to us than just about anything else. All other quality/convenience factors being equal, adding a social dimension can change the prospect of a product or service. That's why teens will buy a cell-phone ring tone for three dollars, but balk at paying ninety-nine cents for a full song on iTunes. A song on your iPod is just for its owner to enjoy—it has little social value. A ring tone announces your taste in music to the world, giving it great social value. This kind of social dimension can increase the fidelity of anything.

Wrecking-ball moments. Every once in a while a new product or service smashes a market sector and starts an entirely new one, resetting the trade-offs people will make between fidelity and convenience. For example, when digital cameras arrived on the scene, they competed in the overall camera market, which included both film and digital versions. By the 2000s, digital cameras had blown apart the film-camera market, creating an entirely new sector dominated by digital cameras on both the high end (or high fidelity) and low end (or high convenience). Film cameras became entombed inside the fidelity belly, offering few advantages in fidelity or convenience for most consumers.

The fidelity/convenience trade-off gives us a new kind of lens for understanding business and, for that matter, other aspects of life. One way to envision how the trade-off works is to put it on a chart.

A product or service that's positioned high up along the fidelity axis might not offer much convenience, but that's okay—customers will make that trade-off of high convenience and low fidelity. Similarly, a product or service far out on the convenience axis doesn't need much fidelity. And, in fact, the most successful products or services tend to be high convenience/low fidelity—or high fidelity/low convenience.

Products or services that are so-so fidelity and so-so convenience wind up in the fidelity belly, a zone of muddy brand vision and consumer apathy.

In the upper-right is the fidelity mirage. I'll explain later why trying to reach the mirage is a fool's errand. Like an invisible tractor beam in a *Star Trek* movie, the dynamics of the fidelity/convenience trade-off drag any entity that drives toward the mirage down toward the fidelity belly.

The arrows at the end of each axis depict the tech effect. Technology constantly moves the outer edges of fidelity and

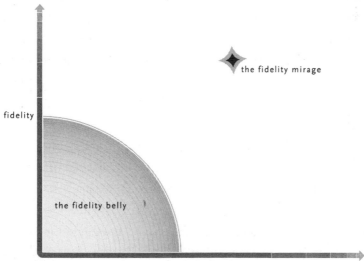

convenience. Products or services that don't adapt get left behind, eventually winding up in the fidelity belly.

/ / /

How can the fidelity-swap model shed new light on a particular product or business? Let's look at the ways to buy a book.

At the top end of fidelity in terms of the book-buying experience are the well-run, well-known, quirky independent bookstores that people will go out of their way to visit, like the Tattered Cover in Denver, Kramerbooks in Washington, D.C., or The Book Stall in Winnetka, Illinois. They're not just bookstores—they are destination locations that have social value. Telling others that you bought a book at the Tattered Cover conveys a bit of status upon you and your tastes. Despite pressure from big bookstore chains, these independent bookstores thrive because of their fidelity advantage.

Over on the convenience axis, at the far end, sits Amazon .com. There is no easier way to learn about and buy a book, and get it into your hands. You don't have to drive anywhere. Features such as Amazon's reader reviews, one-click ordering, high discounts, and free shipping make Amazon today's best bookselling website. It thrives because it is the convenience winner.

So where do other book-selling stores land on the quality/convenience scale? Wal-Mart lands on the convenience side, although it is less convenient than Amazon, because you have to drive there. A Barnes & Noble or Borders superstore, on the other hand, lands on the fidelity side—not on a par, perhaps, with a Tattered Cover, because a Barnes & Noble is a chain and doesn't convey as much of a special experience. Still it offers a good book-buying experience.

Smaller, less distinguished independent bookstores are a dying breed, however, in part because they've fallen inside the fidelity belly. They don't have the selection of Amazon or a chain superstore, or the social aura that would give them the fidelity to lure a sizable base of customers. Nor are they convenient enough—except maybe for people who live down the block— to compete with Amazon or Wal-Mart. Consumers will give up convenience for something that gives them very high fidelity. And large numbers of people will give up fidelity for high convenience. Anything that falls in the fidelity belly just doesn't excite customers that much at either end of the scale.

Another example of the fidelity swap can be seen in the realm of watching sports on television.

The highest-fidelity TV sport in the U.S. market is NFL football. The production values are exquisite. The game in many ways is better seen on television than in the stands—thanks to close-up camera shots, insightful commentary, and instant replay of key plays. There is also a social value to watching pro football on television that's not matched by baseball or basketball or any other sport. People interrupt their lives or get together to watch "the game." At work on Monday, they talk about it. It all contributes to the NFL's fidelity on TV—and football's success on TV is unquestionable.

On the other axis, at the far end of convenience is ESPN— twenty-four hours of sports of all kinds, from game updates to highlights to such niche sports as motocross racing and bass fishing. The fidelity of ESPN isn't high—you never know what might be on when you turn on your TV set, and there is little social value in watching it. But the convenience is phenomenal if all you want is a sports fix. Flick on the channel, and it's there, every time.

One reason the National Hockey League has such trouble getting decent ratings in the United States is that it falls in the fidelity belly. The NHL is not a high-fidelity TV sport. The puck is too small to be seen easily on a screen at home or in a bar. The action and speed are difficult to capture on camera. And production values tend to be weak—hockey is not a big-money sport, so low-budget cable networks don't spend much on production values, which contributes to low ratings. And watching an NHL game has far less social value in the United States than watching an NFL football game. It's not the subject of water-cooler conversation. Nor are NHL games convenient. They are relegated to obscure cable channels in many markets, and games are often unavailable in cities that don't host an NHL team. You have to work to see a hockey game. So the NHL on TV, compared with other major sports, is low on both fidelity and convenience. (Later in the book, I'll discuss how the NHL might use the fidelity/convenience lens to connect with a larger audience.)

This exercise is effective in looking at any industry or market segment. But it also brings up a challenge. A business has to decide which market it's competing in. If you're the head of the NHL thinking about your audience, do you figure the league is competing in the "sports on TV" category, trying to win viewers who might otherwise tune into basketball or competitive poker? Or is the league competing only for the attention of die-hard hockey fans, rather than the casual sports fan? The NHL's decisions about how to manage trade-offs between fidelity and convenience will be different depending on the market it most wants to serve.

Companies have debated about the categories their products or services fall into for decades. In 1952, Justice Department officials wanted to prosecute IBM for antitrust violations. The government argued that IBM completely dominated the punch-card machine market—the computers of the day. CEO Thomas Watson brought a diagram into the meeting that presented a completely different argument. It showed a pyramid redefining the market as the entire range of business calculations. The bottom third was labeled "Pencils and Ledger-Books," the middle third was "Adding Machines, Posting Machines, Bank-Teller Machines," and the smallest piece at the top was "Punch-Card Machines." To the government, IBM was a monopoly. In Watson's view, IBM handled only about 16 percent of the accounting work done in the United States. If IBM just competed in the punch-card bucket, it was so dominant that customers had no ability to make any fidelity/convenience trade-offs—IBM was the only choice. But when viewed through the lens of competing in the broader accounting bucket, customers could choose the low fidelity/high convenience approach of an adding machine over IBM's high-fidelity automated machines.

The act of thinking through a business's "bucket" or category is instructive. It can help managers think about what business they're really in, who they're genuinely competing against, and what trade-offs their customers will make.

/ / /

Several months after writing one of my columns in *USA Today* about fidelity versus convenience, I got an e-mail from Daniel Stevens, who ran the Washington, North Carolina, office of the North Carolina Division of Vocational Rehabilitation. The office helps people with disabilities find jobs locally. It's not an easy task. But the tension I described between fidelity and convenience gave Stevens some ideas of how to better help his clients find jobs.

"Appeals to the heart don't work," Stevens told me when I called to follow up on his e-mail. "I was going through training—the nuts and bolts of how we talk to employers about why they should hire the disabled. It's always been a more sales-oriented approach. But one thing you don't ask is what kind of employee a manager is looking for. They'll describe an ideal employee." Stevens's agency often can't supply an ideal employee. But as Stevens considered his dilemma through the lens of fidelity versus convenience, he told me, "All of a sudden, I saw a parallel between ideal versus real and fidelity versus convenience."

The "ideal" employee is a high-fidelity employee. But high-fidelity employees are hard—i.e., inconvenient—to find. Finding them usually takes time, and a lot of work interviewing and searching. And you have to pay them more to lure them and to keep them. On the other hand, the "real" employee is someone who is ready and available right now. Even if he or she doesn't have every skill an employer might ideally want, the convenience of having a "good enough" prospect who is ready to jump into a much-needed vacancy is often a convenience managers appreciate. It reminded Stevens of something he had heard from Bill Santos, of the employment consulting firm Employment Management Professionals. "Bill told us that timing is key," Stevens says. "You keep going back because if the dishwasher just quit, that's when a manager feels like he needs to hire a dishwasher right away. It ties into convenience."

Although Stevens was always careful to avoid saying people with disabilities couldn't be high-fidelity employees, the truth is that many managers don't see a disabled person in that light. Stevens's agency was trying to sell a product (disabled job-seekers) that customers (business managers) saw as of lesser quality. But the agency's approach didn't focus on the convenience of hiring its clientele. As a result, employers didn't see Stevens's clients as high-convenience either. In the agency's approach, disabled job-seekers fell into the fidelity belly. They were seen as having neither high enough fidelity nor high enough convenience to generate much enthusiasm from employers.

Stevens started encouraging his office to try a different approach, by focusing on convenience. If the Division of Vocational Rehabilitation could become the employment agency of convenience—"we can quickly supply a good-enough employee to your door, ready to work"—it should have more success than when it fell into the gray middle area of so-so convenience and so-so fidelity.

In the summer of 2008, I checked back with Stevens to find out how the new approach was working. "We implemented this one year ago with just a few offices," he wrote in an e-mail. "When compared with their numbers from last year, these offices are having increased success with direct placements, and those placements have increased the instance of successful employment outcomes over the last four to six months."

The quality/convenience trade-off applied even to the employment business. But let me give you an example of how it applied to a decision far removed from Stevens's employment office. This was a decision made by rocker Ozzy Osbourne.

Osbourne grew up in the Aston area of Birmingham, England, and formed a band with his pal, guitarist Tony Iommi. They originally considered naming the band Polka Tulk; to rock history's relief, they eventually settled on Black Sabbath. The band churned out a number of hits in the early 1970s. Osbourne became a drug abuser and was fired from Black Sabbath in 1979, only to resurrect his career as a solo performer. He introduced himself to a whole new generation in the 2000s with his hit reality show about his family. During that time, he created Ozzfest, a touring festival of big-name heavy-metal bands. Ozzfest took off with heavy-metal fans just before online music began to eat away at CD sales. It has gotten more popular since. Ozzfest has taken in more than $100 million in revenue over the years. In 2006, Ozzfest tickets cost $125, and the festivals were consistently jammed.

In early 2007, Osbourne decreed that the wildly popular Ozzfest would be free—recast as FreeFest. Concert ticket prices were too high, Osbourne claimed. Ozzfest would give something back to fans by charging nothing for tickets. It followed that Ozzfest would no longer pay the bands to perform. His argument to the bands? They will get to play before thousands of potential new fans who will then go out and buy the bands' CDs. Except Osbourne seemingly forgot that most young Ozzfest fans rarely bought CDs, and instead often filled their iPods with music downloaded for free from file-sharing sites.

In other words, Osbourne turned the fidelity swap model completely inside-out. Consumer excitement centers around high fidelity or high convenience. In music, a big, boisterous, A-list romp of a music festival is at the top of the fidelity axis— which is why fans will pay $125 to attend. In general, live music is extremely high fidelity—it cannot be replicated in any other way, and in addition has a high social benefit. Jimmy Buffett figured that out years ago. He played twenty-five dates in 2007, for an average ticket price of $136, raking in $35.6 million—up 34 percent from 2006. Most Buffett fans probably haven't bought one of his CDs in years. But they flock to his concerts, donning parrot hats and partying in tailgate festivities that look like scenes from *Girls Gone Wild: Menopause Edition.*

In short, Osbourne had a super-fidelity revenue model for Ozzfest. And he unwittingly threw it away in favor of a revenue model stuck in the middle of the fidelity belly. The first FreeFest, in 2007, was a success, in the sense that thousands attended and the festival still attracted high-level metal bands. But as the bands discover that fans aren't rushing out to buy CDs, they'll discover that playing FreeFest isn't such a great business proposition. Increasingly, the bands that choose to play the festival for nothing will be unknowns hoping to get a toehold among metal fans. As the name recognition and quality of the acts that participate in FreeFest decrease, fewer people will come—even for free.

CHAPTER TWO

Fidelity Versus Convenience

Jeff Bezos leaned back in his chair.[1] We were in a conference room in New York, in the summer of 2008. He had a few more crinkles around the eyes and a little less hair than when he'd started Amazon.com over a decade before. But nobody has ever accused Bezos of losing any of his enthusiasm for his company and his work. His latest point of pride was the Kindle electronic book reader, unveiled in late 2007. After Amazon started the Kindle project in 2004, Bezos and his core team spent months trying to decode the fidelity and convenience around perhaps the most enduring technology in history: the physical book. They wanted to nail down the reason books dominated in the delivery of long-form narratives, stories, and information for 550 years, and why every attempt at an e-book reader so far had failed. Bezos felt that the Kindle cracked the code. It was inconceivable to him that the Kindle might get stuck inside the fidelity belly—and that Amazon had to find a way out. He pointed out that the Kindle had sizzling sales in its first six months and glowing reviews. But it seemed that the Kindle—like a lot of early technologies—had started life without either the convenience or the fidelity to light a fire under a sizable market.

While trying to dissect and analyze the paper book, the Amazon team focused on a book's fidelity—although the team didn't use the term. The team wanted to figure out why the experience of reading a book felt so good to so many people. "We even got into how books smell," Bezos said. "We did research, and found that the smell is mostly glue—glue and maybe mildew. We joked that maybe we should have a spritzer on the [Kindle] that would send out that smell. Why do people like the smell of glue and mildew? Because they associate it with being inside the author's world." All in all, the team found that trying to improve on the book "was one of the most absurd challenges," Bezos said.

After months of meetings, the team agreed on one particular concept that they felt rang true: the best thing about a book is that it disappears. You start reading, and you don't notice the physical book itself, just the words and ideas on the page. The book gets out of the way of its content. "That became the top design objective of the Kindle—to make it disappear," Bezos said. "So three years ago, we said we have to make sure the device gets out of the way just like a physical book so you can lose yourself, but at the same time you've got to find some things that you could never do with a physical book, and we have to do those things amazingly well." The team knew that it couldn't just *match* physical books—the Kindle had to be *better* than a book on some significant level. Otherwise few consumers would consider switching to an e-book reader.

The result was an intriguing device. The first Kindle used an E-Ink screen that looked more like the flat, solid print of ink on paper than characters on an electronic screen. It weighed 10.3 ounces and had a six-inch-wide screen, so it was about the size and weight of a paperback book. Levers on the side were supposed to make it natural and easy to flip through pages. As for its overall look, Amazon was going for an "aura of bookishness," Bezos said—and the Kindle somewhat achieved it. Although, of course, the glue-and-mildew smell was missing.

To beat the book—to be *better* than a book—Amazon built the Kindle to be a wireless communication device. That way, it could download e-books, newspapers, magazines, and blogs anywhere, anytime. "It isn't a device," Bezos commented. "It's a service." The wireless connectivity also allowed a Kindle user to look up a word or concept right from the e-book, jumping to Wikipedia or an online dictionary. Notes scribbled in margins on the Kindle could be saved not only on Kindle, but on Amazon's computers, allegedly forever. When the Kindle launched, it had access to about 90,000 books, nearly all priced at $9.99—far less than hardcover list prices, though only somewhat better than Amazon's discount prices. Bezos's goal was to make millions of titles available for the Kindle. "The vision for Kindle is that any book, in any language, ever in print should be available in less than sixty seconds," Bezos told me.

The Kindle seemed to be striving to achieve both better fidelity and better convenience than a book. But then you get to the factors that complicated the Kindle's fidelity/convenience equation. One was Kindle's price. At $399, the Kindle is not very convenient for most people. On the fidelity side, Kindle was on shaky ground as well. I'll explain in a moment. But all in all, while the Kindle sold out in its first incarnation, many of those first customers were not the mass-market reading public, but well-off early adopters who enjoyed buying new gadgets and toys. The fidelity/convenience equation suggests that the Kindle will have trouble breaking out, unless Amazon changes the device and how it's marketed in key ways.

/ / /

To better understand the natural tension between fidelity and convenience, it's helpful to look at how, why, and when people shift from being attracted to fidelity to being drawn to convenience, and back again, in their everyday lives.

What Is Fidelity?

The broadest, simplest definition of fidelity is that it is the total experience of something.

High fidelity is the best, most pleasing, most sensory experience possible. Price is relatively unimportant. Think about what makes up a great experience. Apply it to, say, a college education. There are lots of ways to get a college education, from paying $50,000 a year in tuition, room, and board to attend a well-known private college, to attending night school part-time at your local community college, to taking online courses from the University of Phoenix. A large chunk of the potential college population chooses to spend a premium to attend a prestigious school. They want to interact with their professors in person, engage in campus life, go to the football games, and find their way among like-minded people. A campus like Harvard or Duke or Stanford is a fantastically high-fidelity version of higher education.

Just about everything has a high-fidelity manifestation. Take men's suits. The most high-fidelity or high-quality version would be a suit custom-made by an expert tailor. Not only do you get a suit that fits perfectly and is exactly what you want, but the making of the suit becomes wrapped in the singular experience of getting measured, choosing materials, and working with the tailor. Let's look at another product—cell phones. In 2008, the highest-fidelity cell phone was Apple's 3G iPhone. It was well ahead of every other phone in the way it looked and worked, and it was among the first to have both cellular capabilities and Wi-Fi. The iPhone also cost more than almost any other cell phone when first introduced, about $600. By comparison, low-fidelity cell phones—the base models—are offered by carriers for free when you sign up for a new account or get an upgrade.

Only the most basic commodities lack a high-fidelity version. You'd be hard-pressed, for example, to find high-fidelity electricity.

High fidelity often means the most expensive product or service—but not always. Earlier, I discussed sports on TV—and argued that NFL games sit at the top of the fidelity axis, while ESPN comes in as lower in fidelity but high in convenience. Consumers actually pay *less* to see an NFL game on a major TV network (which can be tuned in for free over-the-air) than to watch ESPN (which you can only get if you buy a cable or satellite TV package). In other words, fidelity is about the experience, rather than the cost, although in many cases you pay a premium for a high-quality, high-fidelity experience.

Fidelity is often about tactile, visible, sensory aspects of a product or service. But fidelity is also made up of two subtle components that can be easy to overlook: *aura* and *identity*.

Walter Benjamin, a German cultural critic who was particularly active in the 1930s, described the idea of aura in his 1936 essay "The Work of Art in the Age of Mechanical Reproduction."[2] The essay is often cited in academic discussions about the real value of music when digital copies of recorded songs can be made and sent around on the Internet for basically no cost. Art, music, words, and images were not digital in Benjamin's day, but he foresaw an era when a work of art—especially a painting—could be perfectly reproduced by a machine. This made him wonder why an original work would be more valuable than a perfect copy. If the value of a painting was strictly in looking at it, then the original should be worth no more than an exact copy. But there is another, unseen value to the original—a sense of awe and reverence for the work, the artist, and the painting's cultural significance. Benjamin called that its *aura*. Fast-forward to today's music business; there is really no aura attached to recorded music on a CD or on the Internet. Aura only comes into play in the context of live concerts. It's the reason people still pay $50 or $100 or more to attend a live concert, even when they won't pay $15 for a CD. The aura of seeing a performer live—the powerful authenticity of seeing the real person perform in real time—adds a huge amount to the fidelity of the experience.

Aura can add to the fidelity of a lot of products. There is certainly an aura to attending Harvard and other prestigious universities. There is an aura to a handmade suit—particularly if it comes from a famous tailor or well-known neighborhood, like London's Savile Row. There is an aura to a copy of a physical book signed by the author. The mass-produced iPhone had an aura in its first few months, when iPhones were very difficult to get. But that aura faded as iPhones became readily available. In some product or service categories, aura plays a negligible role. There is not much aura pulling people to a particular convenience store chain.

Aura is sometimes based entirely on perceptions and marketing—a kind of perceived fidelity. A certain restaurant may be seen as "hot," even though the food might be better at five others nearby. An interesting example of perceived fidelity can be seen in a product called Monster Cables. Monster makes audio cables for stereo systems and musical instruments. It positions and markets itself as an ultra-premium brand. A cable that might cost twenty dollars from most manufacturers will cost sixty dollars from Monster. The Monster products do well because consumers think the music that comes through their speakers sounds better because of the quality of the Monster Cables. But when the website Engadget did a blindfold test with self-professed audiophiles, the audio experts couldn't tell the difference between music played through Monster Cables and the music played on the same system but using coat hangers to connect the speakers to the amplifier.[3]

Perceived fidelity can be a powerful marketing tool, but it can be transient in nature. As soon as people decide a restaurant is no longer hot, or that Monster Cables are just marketing hype, that aura will deflate and go away.

The second aspect of fidelity that is easy to overlook is identity. Many of our consumer choices are a way to tell other people something about ourselves. This is particularly true when making high-fidelity choices. We perceive that something has more fidelity if it tells other people something unique and significant about us—if it gives us a certain social cachet.

Certainly this is a huge factor in the fidelity of attending Harvard or any other well-known university. Where you go to school becomes part of your identity. It signals a lot about who you are, what you accomplished, and where you fit in. The ability to say "I went to Harvard" is, for many, probably worth more than the actual experience of going to Harvard. This is part of the reason why attending Harvard is a higher-fidelity education experience than attending, say, Penn State: the identity aspect of Harvard is worth more.

The concept of identity applies to a broad spectrum of things. Part of the fidelity of the hand-tailored suit is the social cachet it gives its owner. By contrast, an off-the-rack suit from Men's Wearhouse has very little cachet. Owning an iPhone in 2007–2008 helped to identify you as a savvy, early adopter of cool technology. A free Samsung cell phone said nothing like that about you. As car manufacturers know, car-buying decisions are based as much on personal identity as on practical matters like gas mileage or luggage space. Clothes play an oversized role in establishing one's identity—whether it's owning the cool new brand of sneakers, jeans from a hot designer, or a T-shirt emblazoned with the name of a favorite band. The more an item says about your identity, the more fidelity it has for you.

Identity is a reason consumers will spend money on live music, but not on recorded music. There is little identity in owning a CD or downloaded song by your favorite band (although there is, no doubt, some identity in playing a hot new CD loudly in your car as you drive past your friends). But going to a concert has a big identity component. By merely going, "you identify yourself as someone who has a relationship with that artist," says Mary Davis, a music historian at Case Western University. "It puts you in a community of like-minded people. It says something about you."[4] People talk the rest of their lives about the concerts they've been to. Being able to say, "Yeah, I saw The Clash when they played on Broadway in New York in 1981," carries a certain social cachet, which increases the value—the fidelity—of going to a live show.

So, back to Amazon's Kindle: the device misses a critical

identity component. Books are identity markers. Pulling out a particular book on an airline flight or in a doctor's office signals something about you. Books that convey a positive sense of who we are and what our tastes are like help us broadcast information about ourselves that we would like others to have. Books lining a living room or office bookshelf tell others a great deal about you. The collection of books you've read and bought and thought to display helps convey a sense of your identity to others. As a result, the outward-facing aspect of a book—the jacket and physical book itself—is a vital part of the fidelity of a book, especially for avid book readers. And avid book readers are the primary target for Amazon's Kindle. No one can see what book you're reading on a Kindle on the plane. Your virtual bookshelf sits on an Amazon computer. Presumably it could be shared online—Amazon would be smart to allow, say, a Facebook profile to show your Kindle e-book shelf. But for most book readers, a virtual bookshelf will fall far short of the fidelity of a real bookshelf. And it's all because of identity.

Experience plus aura plus identity equals fidelity.

What Is Convenience?

Convenience refers to how easy it is to get something.

The easiest way to consume music in the late 2000s is through iTunes and iPods. There are several reasons for that. One is that, because the store is on the Net, you can buy pretty much any song you want at any time from wherever you happen to be. In other words, availability is a factor in convenience. This alone gives iTunes a convenience advantage over a physical music store. If iTunes happened to be difficult or frustrating to use, it might not be more convenient than buying a CD at a store. Convenience is ultimately about the ease of getting the result you want. But Apple has made iTunes and the iPod exceptionally easy to use, automatically doing much of the work of downloading a song, putting it in the iTunes player on your PC, and transferring it into your iPod. Once the music is in iTunes, or on an iPod, listening to it is as easy as sliding a disk into a CD player. An iPod, though, beats CDs on convenience because it lets you carry around hundreds or thousands of CDs' worth of music in your pocket. (As Apple illustrates, it's possible for one company to have a portfolio that includes both high fidelity—the iPhone— and high convenience—the iPod.)

Any factor that makes something easier to obtain relative to its competition makes that product or service more convenient. In the category of "cooking at home," a microwavable meal is far more convenient than a meal that requires preparation and cooking. You take it out of the box and stick it in the microwave for a few minutes. The microwavable version is simpler, more foolproof, and takes less time. In the 1960s, in the category of making copies of documents, Xerox copiers set a new standard for convenience. Making a copy by pushing a button on a Xerox copying machine became quicker, less messy, and produced less frustrating results than making carbon copies on a typewriter, or running off copies on a mimeograph machine.

But ease alone doesn't necessarily make something more convenient than its competitors. There is another critical, and perhaps counterintuitive, factor to convenience. And that is cost.

Cost is a key part of convenience for the simple reason that if something costs less, it is easier for most people to buy—

which means the product or service is easier to obtain. It's less painful—and thus more convenient—to buy a song you really like for ninety-nine cents than to pay fifteen dollars for the whole CD to get that song, or to spend $150 to go to the concert. Southwest Airlines fills its airplanes by offering cheaper prices than its competitors, making flights easier to get for most people—in other words, making flights more convenient.

"Paying for convenience," by the way, is something of a misnomer. Let's say you're in Manhattan and you have to get to a meeting across town. By my definition, the most convenient way to get there would be to walk: readily available, very low cost, easy to do. You just move your legs. Another way to get there would be to call a car service and have them pick you up at your door and deliver you to your destination. This might sound more convenient—but it's really a high-fidelity luxury. You pay a premium to get there in the comfort of the hired car. You're paying for a much better total experience in getting where you have to go. Most of the time, when we find ourselves "paying for convenience," we are really "paying for fidelity."

When you add together ease and cost, you get a sense of overall convenience. In general merchandising, Wal-Mart makes shopping easy by building stores everywhere and packing lots of items into the stores, all at low prices. Wal-Mart is the leader in super-convenient retailing. In higher education, the University of Phoenix puts its courses online for a fraction of the cost of traditional college courses, making it a highly convenient adult educator. Apple has become the super-convenient legitimate music retailer—topped in convenience only by the illegal downloading and trading of songs for free on file-sharing sites (which dwarf iTunes in number of transactions). All in all, the company that makes it the easiest for consumers to get what they want is hard to beat. That's the power of convenience.

Identity and aura play little or no part in convenience. Often the opposite is true—the most convenient product or service is practically devoid of identity or aura. Think of Wal-Mart. Buying something at Wal-Mart conveys no aura whatsoever. Few people brag about shopping at Wal-Mart as a way to gain social cachet.

And I believe that it is on convenience that Amazon can win with Kindle. The device may never beat the fidelity of books. But new technology can often offer better convenience. Amazon's best strategy might be to make Kindle the super-convenient version of the book.

The Tech Effect

Fidelity and convenience refuse to sit still.

Technology and innovation are constantly moving the borders of both fidelity and convenience. So if you offer the highest-fidelity product or service today, some competitor will come up with new technology or an innovative twist to leap past it. The same is true on the convenience axis. The borders of fidelity and convenience move with time, and consumers are constantly adjusting or changing their standards for each. A product or service that doesn't constantly improve its convenience or fidelity will get left behind.

In the 1920s, the highest-fidelity movie you could see would have been a silent picture. By the 1930s, technology had moved the fidelity border outward. The highest-fidelity movies by then were talkies—films with music and dialogue. By 1939 the highest-fidelity movies were in color. Over the following years, technology pushed the border farther out with surround-sound, then computer-generated special effects. Similarly, over the years, technology and innovation have created new highest-fidelity snow skis, new highest-fidelity TV sets, cameras, cars, and more. In some categories—kitchen utensils, lawn mowers—fidelity has expanded slowly. In others that are more technologically intensive, like cell phones, fidelity shoots ahead like a rocket. No matter what the category, though, technology and innovation continually push out the boundaries of fidelity over time.

On the convenience axis, the pattern is similar. Newspapers were the most convenient way to get written news until websites came along. Driving to Blockbuster was the most convenient way to rent a movie until Netflix's mail-based business model. Pay phones were the most convenient way to make a call when on the road until cell phones. Standing in line at the bank was the most convenient way to get cash until the rise of the ATM. In rural America, driving from one specialty shop to another (hardware store, toy shop, bakery, electronics store) was the most convenient way to shop, until Wal-Mart's superstores came to town, and consumers could do their grocery and other shopping in one location.

The tech effect is sometimes smooth and sometimes "chunky." The more intensely a category relies on information technology, the more its rate of change seems constant and rapid.

Categories less reliant on technology might not budge much on the fidelity or convenience axis for years, only to lurch suddenly forward. One such category is vegetables from the grocery store.

Clarence Birdseye was born in Brooklyn, New York, in 1886. But he spent a lot of time on his family's farm on Long Island, where he developed an odd hobby for a New Yorker: taxidermy. While he attended college, he earned money by trapping and selling rats to a research lab. This in turn led him into a job as a naturalist for the U.S. government, and Birdseye began experimenting with unusual meat dishes—like chipmunk soup. Eventually, Birdseye moved to Labrador, in Canada's northwestern corner. He watched Eskimos catch fish and toss them on the ice, where the fish quickly froze. Birdseye noticed that when thawed, the flash-frozen fish retained their flavor and texture. That gave Birdseye an idea.

In 1924, after experimenting by flash-freezing fish between cakes of dry ice, he started General Seafoods, and developed an entire frozen-foods infrastructure: the technology to freeze foods, freezer cases for grocers to house the vegetables, and freezer cars for railroads to transport them. He applied the technology to vegetables, and by the 1940s, Birdseye was selling frozen vegetables to consumers.

Birdseye's approach was a fidelity play. Before then, if it wasn't harvest time, fresh vegetables just weren't available for most families. The highest-fidelity "vegetables at home" out of season came in a can or jar. And canned veggies tasted nothing like fresh vegetables. The first ads for what Birdseye called frosted foods—under the familiar Bird's Eye brand—pitched them as luxury products. One *Life* magazine ad showed a woman in pearls lounging on a pillow eating Bird's Eye spinach, implying that only commoners put up with canned spinach. Birdseye had vaulted the fidelity axis for home produce forward, changing the dynamics of the whole food industry.

/ / /

Ted Leonsis is part businessman, and part philosopher. I first got to know him in 1991 when he ran Redgate Communications, one of the first interactive marketing companies. Leonsis was thinking about Internet-style marketing before there was a mass-market Internet. In 1993, Redgate became the first company bought by what was then a fast-growing dynamo called America Online. Leonsis got absorbed into AOL and eventually became president. During AOL's most dynamic period, the company was run by Leonsis, Bob Pittman, and CEO Steve Case. The venture made Leonsis a very wealthy man. He bought the Washington Capitals hockey team in 1999, produced film documentaries in the 2000s, and continues to invest in tech startups.

Leonsis told me about a mantra that has guided him through-out his career—a little saying that has helped him evaluate busi-ness opportunities: A successful business is either loved or needed.[5]

My conversations with Leonsis about companies that are "loved or needed" added texture to my ideas about fidelity and convenience. Fidelity is all about being loved (although not nec-essarily needed). Designer clothes, rock concerts, iPhones, Tif-fany's jewelry, Prada bags, lie-flat first-class airline seats—they're all loved, but rarely needed. They are high-fidelity but not conve-nient.

Convenience, on the other hand, is about being needed. Wal-Mart, microwave ovens, 7-Eleven, and inexpensive home com-puters have all become needed. (This is how the tech effect can change things. In 1983, almost no one saw a home computer as a necessity, according to a survey by Pew Research Center. By 2006, about 50 percent of the population thought it was a ne-cessity.)[6] While such things might be needed by a lot of people, they're not usually *loved,* any more than toilet paper or dish detergent is loved. And these products don't need to be loved to succeed.

High-fidelity products or services often occupy a high-end niche. They are relatively expensive, but have fewer customers. In fact, part of their fidelity has to do with their exclusivity, because it is their exclusivity that lends them social cachet and identity. On the flip side, high-convenience products or services often serve the mass market. They cost relatively little but touch almost everyone. The mass appeal adds to the convenience because it tends to make the product or service more available and drive the price even lower. The mass appeal also diminishes the fidelity of a product or service—because if everyone has it or does it, it doesn't do anything to boost our sense of identity.

Both successful high-fidelity products or services and successful high-convenience products can be great businesses. They are just different kinds of businesses.

But it's very hard to be both loved and needed, to be both high-fidelity and high-convenience. In fact, trying to achieve both can lead to a breakdown.

/ / /

What does all this say about Jeff Bezos's Kindle? The fidelity/convenience trade-off suggests that electronic books will have a hard time beating the fidelity of physical books—just as MP3s can't beat the fidelity of a CD. However, e-books can beat the pants off the convenience of physical books, and that is the path MP3s have followed to beat CDs.

Amazon.com's Kindle—as marketed in 2008—was still in

no-man's-land. The company was trying to give it both higher fidelity and higher convenience compared to a book. Instead, the Kindle was halfway between the two in both directions.

To shoot for the mass market, Amazon would have to pour its resources into making the Kindle super-convenient. Bezos already has the right approach: to make every book available within sixty seconds. It would be the most convenient bookstore ever. But cost is part of convenience, too. That suggests that the Kindle needs to dramatically drop in price. True, people pay a couple hundred dollars for an iPod—but music lovers always needed some kind of device to play music, whether a portable CD player or a Walkman tape player or a home stereo. No one has ever had to buy a device to read a book. Paying $300 or more for a device to read books seems highly inconvenient, unless the books are radically cheaper in price than the paper versions. If the cost of a Kindle drops to near nothing and the ease of buying and storing books on it can blast past the convenience of buying and lugging around physical books, consumers might discover they're willing to trade a paper book's fidelity for the Kindle's convenience.

Navigating that kind of trade-off is where marketing magic lies.

CHAPTER THREE

The Trade-Off, the Belly,
and the Mirage

Over Christmas break in 2007, my son, Sam, then about to turn fourteen, was visiting relatives 3,000 miles from home when he got a text message on his cell phone bearing devastating news. His friend and soccer teammate had been killed in a car crash. Sam's circle of friends suddenly had to deal with a death among them, and they reached out to one another for support and comfort. The way they did it—especially with Sam, since he was so far away—was through text messages. Lots and lots and lots of text messages. When I looked at the cell-phone statement a month later, I couldn't believe it. During that time, Sam sent or received more than 400 texts a day. If you subtract time to sleep, eat, and use the bathroom, he averaged about one text every two minutes.

Why text messages? It's just text on a tiny screen—not pictures or graphics. And they have a limit of 160 characters. It's pretty much the lowest-fidelity form of human communication possible, unless you count smoke signals and Morse code. Sam could have used instant messaging or e-mail, or just dialed his cell phone and called his friends. He could've gone higher fidelity and used a webcam to set up a video conference over the Internet. But in Sam's social group—eighth graders who have their own cell phones—text messaging is the winner in convenience. The cell phone sits in your pocket all day long. Access is instantaneous. There is no booting up or signing into anything, and no having to stop what you're doing to take a voice phone call. You can either quietly answer a text right when it arrives, or do it at the next available opportunity. Middle-aged adults would no doubt make different choices, probably preferring to talk on the phone. Yet Sam and his friends favored swapping the fidelity of any other form of communication for the convenience of texting.

A different social group—high-level technology managers—prefers a very different set of trade-offs when interacting with other humans. IBM, like many corporate giants, has offices all over the world. IBM engineers and technical staff often have to work on projects with colleagues spread from Silicon Valley to New York, Germany, and China. They can't always get on airplanes each time they need to talk—the highest-fidelity solution. For decades they relied on conference calls. The IBMers, though, discovered another option: meeting in the virtual world called Second Life. Members of a technical team can each have an avatar—a cartoonish depiction of themselves—in Second Life. To hold a meeting, they each guide their own avatar into a predetermined "room." This place might look like a conference room with a table and chairs, or it might look like no meeting space you've ever seen, with strange chairs, no walls, and art hanging in midair. As the IBM avatars gather, each can see the other avatars, and the effect is much like when people start to trickle into a traditional meeting room. Attendees can chitchat by typing on their keyboards. They can move across the room to great an old friend. And when they all sit down to get to work, the meeting dynamics seem more like a face-to-face meeting than a conference call. In fact, IBM has begun encouraging Second Life meetings because people find them more engaging and productive than conference calls.

"Let's assume there are twenty people meeting, or even ten," says Irving Wladawsky-Berger, who ran IBM's technology strategy in the early 2000s and promoted Second Life within the company. "In a conference call, no one knows who's talking. It's very impersonal. A characteristic of a physical meeting is people chat before and after. Conference calls don't do that. In virtual worlds, it feels more like a real meeting."[1]

Now, here's the rub: Second Life in the late 2000s could be difficult to navigate for the average person—even someone moderately tech-savvy. For the majority of the population, meeting in Second Life was not at all convenient because it violated that important rule of convenience: it must be easy. By comparison, conference calls were just about the easiest—and thus most convenient—way for a dispersed group of people to talk at once. But to the kind of person who works as a technical staffer at IBM, navigating Second Life came easily, and Second Life's fidelity was better than a conference call. When it comes to conference calls, IBM tech types work off a different set of fidelity/convenience values than, say, auto parts salesmen in Dallas or eighth graders in U.S. suburbs. In the category of meetings, IBM tech types will trade the convenience of a conference call for the slightly lower convenience but higher fidelity of a Second Life meeting.

People constantly swap fidelity for convenience, and vice versa. It's a decision we make all the time, every day.

That trade-off is the engine of the fidelity swap. People make different decisions depending on the situation. Not all people make the same decisions in the same situations. Middle-class eighth graders opt for texting over voice calls, when their parents would rarely make that trade. Engineers at IBM choose virtual-world meetings over conference calls, while employees at less tech-savvy companies would not. Figuring out how different groups define fidelity and convenience can help identify target markets, and lend insight into the successes and failures of all kinds of products.

The Trade-Off

The fidelity swap is an individual's decision to trade fidelity for convenience or vice versa.

This is easy to see in everyday life. Listening to a U2 song wherever you happen to be on an iPod, rather than on a surround-sound system at home, is a decision based on convenience over fidelity. Going to a U2 concert is a trade for fidelity over convenience. Popping into McDonald's on a long trip is a choice for convenience. Going to a four-star restaurant is a choice for fidelity.

Fidelity/convenience trade-offs are often based on a situation. If you're in a hurry, you'll choose the convenience of McDonald's, even if a high-fidelity gourmet restaurant sits next door.

And trade-offs can vary among different demographics.

In mid-2008, a survey by the National Center for Health Statistics showed that 34.5 percent of people twenty-five to twenty-nine years old lived in a household with no land-line phone, served only by cell phones. For people thirty to forty-four years old, 15.5 percent went wireless only. For those over sixty-five, just 2.2 percent ditched their land lines.[2] When it comes to home phones, people in their twenties have completely different trade-off tendencies from people over sixty-five. In "making and receiving voice calls while at home," a land-line phone is actually a pretty high-fidelity solution. It's extremely reliable, never drops calls, can feed an incoming call into multiple handsets at once, and has 911 service that tracks the address of the calling party. Land-line phones are also quite expensive compared with, say, making Internet-based calls on Skype. In contrast, cell phones are actually a convenient solution for a lot of people. By the mid-2000s, almost every person of at least modest means had a cell phone. Increasingly, people felt that if they already had a cell for mobile calling, why not use it at home, too? The cost of adding home calls was essentially zero—because you already had the phone and the calling plan. That made the cell phone more convenient on cost than a land line. Plus the cell offered other conveniences, like making it easier to get phone calls—every call would reach the phone's owner wherever he or she happened to be. But cell calls cannot be called high fidelity. The reception can be sketchy, and the voice quality rarely matches that of a land-line phone.

Those surveyed who were over sixty-five valued the fidelity of a land-line phone far more than the convenience of going wireless only. People in their twenties, though, valued wireless convenience far more than wired fidelity.

How does age play out in other ways? Take the real estate business. The highest-fidelity way to look for a house or condo—the way that engages all your senses—is to see the house in person with a real estate agent. The most convenient solution is to search online, something you can do anywhere, at any time. But the text and photos (and even the occasional video) can't match the fidelity of walking around a property with an agent. A 2006 survey by the Pew Internet & American Life Project found that 51 percent of Americans eighteen to twenty-nine years old searched online for housing information. In other words, they chose convenience first. Of Internet users sixty-five and older (only those of that age who go on the Net) just 15 percent searched online for housing information.[3]

Those two examples might make you think that young people always tend to decide in favor of convenience over fidelity, while older people prefer fidelity over convenience, but such a conclusion is overly simplistic. Another Pew study looked at products that people said they "need." The results for microwave ovens, for example, are interesting. In cooking at home, microwaves have the highest convenience, while cooking from scratch on a stove or in an oven would be the highest fidelity. The age breakdowns, though, are surprising. Among respondents eighteen to twenty-nine, 72 percent believed they must have a microwave. For ages thirty to forty-nine, only 61 percent felt they needed a microwave. But among the over-sixty-five set, 75 percent felt they needed a microwave—a higher percentage than those in their twenties.[4] Why? The youngest and the oldest age brackets are more likely making meals for just themselves, or themselves and a spouse. The middle age brackets are more likely to be making meals for their families. If you're cooking for one or two, the convenience of a microwave is desirable. If you're cooking for a family, you might be more likely to go for the fidelity of making a "real" dinner on the stove.

Such trade-off decisions often differ by income, as well. Cost is a significant factor in convenience. As a result, convenience is going to mean one thing to someone who makes $200,000 a year and another thing to someone who makes $50,000 a year. You'd expect a more affluent person to tend more toward fidelity—designer clothes, shopping at high-service boutiques, buying front-row concert seats. People in the lower income brackets are likely to tend toward convenience, to save money. They buy clothes off the rack, shop at Wal-Mart, and only hear their favorite bands through earbuds.

In the aggregate, patterns tend to emerge in fidelity/convenience trade-offs. People tend to choose the most convenient product or service most of the time but treat themselves to fidelity. To go back to Ted Leonsis's observation: convenience is needed; fidelity is loved.

No-Man's-Land

Any product or service that offers too little of either convenience or fidelity risks landing below a threshold where consumers are motivated to act. I call that threshold the fidelity belly.

In mid-2006, as a growing number of households were buying high-definition televisions, two competing versions of high-definition video disks—essentially next-generation DVDs—landed on the market. One was Blu-ray, from a group of companies led by Sony. The other was HD-DVD, from a group led by Toshiba. The pitch to consumers was that movies on those disks would look sharper and richer than DVDs when played on HDTVs. Yet over the following eighteen months, sales of Blu-ray and HD-DVD players and disks in both formats were dismal.

The video players cost three or four times more than DVD players, and a movie on a Blu-ray or HD-DVD disk cost twice as much as one on DVD. But the real problem, analysts said at the time, was that the market was poisoned by the format war. Consumers didn't want to buy one kind of player and then get stuck with obsolete technology if that player got booted out of the market, à la Sony's Betamax in the 1980s.

An end to the format war should've popped the cork on consumer demand. In February 2008, HD-DVD bowed out, leaving the market to Blu-ray. The electronics industry thought consumers were going to come out of the woodwork to buy Blu-ray. But that didn't happen. In that first month, sales of Blu-ray players rose only 2 percent, and it didn't seem to get any better in the months after. Most consumers had no interest in laying out a lot more money to switch to Blu-ray, when they already had a perfectly acceptable DVD player and lots of movies on DVD.

Blu-ray in 2008 got stuck inside the fidelity belly. Blu-ray was certainly not more convenient than DVD. It cost more, far fewer movies were available in Blu-ray format, and rental outfits like Netflix and Blockbuster carried few if any Blu-ray titles. In addition, according to the Consumer Electronics Association, 84 percent of all adults already owned a DVD player. (Already owning the necessary equipment makes it very convenient!) On the fidelity side, Blu-ray certainly is better than DVD—but not enough better to make people run out and buy Blu-ray. In the 1990s, DVDs offered a huge improvement in terms of the quality of picture and quality of experience, compared with VHS tapes. Blu-ray enjoys no such fidelity advantage. Few consumers were willing to pay twice as much for a format that offered so few advantages.

For the time being, in the category of "watching movies at

home," DVDs enjoy a position of high convenience and good enough fidelity to keep most viewers happy. A new format could win consumers by offering a vast fidelity improvement (3-D disks?). Blu-ray, though, will have a hard time ever getting out of the fidelity belly. It has little hope of improving the viewing experience significantly compared with DVDs. Its only hope is for the Blu-ray players and movies to become nearly as cheap and available as DVDs, so that the Blu-ray and DVD technologies are about even in convenience. At that point Blu-ray's better fidelity might be enough to persuade masses of consumers to switch.

New technologies, like Blu-ray and Amazon's Kindle, almost always start out *inside the fidelity belly*. They're often too expensive or hard to use to be highly convenient, and they don't yet offer a rich enough experience to win over enough people on fidelity alone. Bill Gross, founder of tech incubator Idealab, operates on the principle that a new technology has to be ten times the fidelity or ten times the convenience of an entrenched product just to get the public's attention.[5] It's hard to find new technologies that meet the criteria early in their existence. Digital cameras, HDTV, personal computers, cell phones, microwave ovens, home air conditioners—all started inside the fidelity belly.

Technologies that never escape the fidelity belly die. These failed technologies are usually referred to as "bad ideas." Blu-ray seems destined to be another bad idea.

The Fidelity Mirage

If consumers love fidelity, and need convenience, one would think that the marriage of the two—high fidelity and high convenience—would be product nirvana. Why not strive to make something that's both loved *and* needed? In fact, that tempting combination is a mirage—try to get there, and you'll find it doesn't exist.

The fidelity mirage helps explain why the fortunes of handbag maker Coach, which soared in the early 2000s, crashed to earth in 2008. The company had been around since the 1970s, making luxury bags and winning the same kind of luxury brand-name recognition as Louis Vuitton and Hermès. In the late 1990s, Coach essentially invented the "accessible luxury" category—launching a strategy to make chic designer bags that would be sold to the mass market. The company had had huge success as a high-fidelity brand, but it wanted to win on both high fidelity and high convenience.

For a number of years in the mid-2000s, the strategy seemed to work. From 2004 to early 2008, Coach opened ninety-four new stores and dozens of discount outlet stores. It made Coach-labeled bags that cost as little as twenty-five dollars. An average Coach bag cost about $300—half the cost of the cheapest bag by luxury competitors such as Vuitton, and far less than anything you could buy from Hermès. Coach opened stores not just in swank locations like Rodeo Drive in Beverly Hills and Fifth Avenue in New York, but in working-class cities like Allentown, Pennsylvania.

A big part of fidelity is derived from a product's aura and identity, and that's particularly true in the fashion industry. Why else would wealthy people pay $20,000 for an Hermès bag? An Hermès bag can't be 1,000 times better than a bag from Target. What Hermès has is cachet—owning an Hermès bag makes a statement about your tastes and income. It is all about aura and identity.

Convenience acts like antimatter to aura and identity. The

more convenient something becomes—the easier it is to get and buy—the more its aura and allure dissipate. The more convenient something becomes, the less that item helps identify its owner as someone who is special and unique.

The very act of pursuing convenience diluted Coach's brand name. By chasing both high fidelity and high convenience, it had become neither. It fell into the fidelity belly. Coach was no longer seen as luxurious, but it wasn't truly mass-market, either. It became neither loved nor needed. Around 2007–8, same-store sales dipped for the first time in years. The stock price had increased 2,000 percent in the early 2000s, as Coach expanded quickly and sold its high-fidelity bags to ever more consumers before the convenience factor wore away at the brand's aura and identity. Once consumers realized Coach was no longer special, they became ambivalent about buying Coach bags. Coach's competitors derided it as the McDonald's of luxury—an oxymoron that perfectly captured Coach's dilemma.

On the flip side, if convenience is all about ease and cost, adding fidelity reduces convenience. Fidelity is about the richness and quality of an experience. Injecting those qualities into a highly available, low-priced product or service usually means adding features and cost. By their very nature, the qualities that add to fidelity take away from convenience. Trying to move from high convenience toward high fidelity, a product or service will fall into the fidelity belly, just like Coach. McDonald's has on several occasions tried creating McDonald's-branded sit-down restaurants, with tablecloths and waiters. All have failed. The McDonald's brand can't move toward fidelity without diluting the very reason people go to the company's restaurants—its high convenience.

As we'll see in coming chapters, however, the fidelity mirage doesn't mean that successful products and services are *only* high-convenience or high-fidelity. In fact, adding the right touch of fidelity to a high-convenience product or service, or the right touch of convenience to fidelity, can make for a powerful, competitor-beating concoction. The trick is to avoid getting greedy and foolishly chasing the mirage.

CHAPTER FOUR

When Andy Grove
Meets Trip Hawkins

Fans of the original *Star Trek* TV show give it kudos for getting the future right. But those beam-me-up-Scotty communicators? They had no camera, no way for Kirk to sneak a shot of Spock petting a Tribble. And that's a major oversight.

Until the early 2000s, it was not obvious that most people wanted a cell phone married to a camera. But once the combination was fully unleashed, the camera phone triggered a wrecking-ball moment in the picture-taking industry. It was one of those rare innovations that slams the marketplace so hard, it disrupts everything around it. Camera phones didn't just occupy a new place among the fidelity trade-offs in the picture-taking industry—it wrecked the old set of trade-offs and created new ones.

Andy Grove, the legendary former CEO of Intel, called such wrecking-ball moments "strategic inflection points"—those times when a new force dramatically alters an industry. When the personal computer for the first time put computing into the hands of everyday consumers, as opposed to back-office professionals—that was a strategic inflection point. The arrival of television, the Internet, and even Clarence Birdseye's frozen foods were other such moments. Grove looked at the phenomenon from a business point of view. The fidelity trade-off turns the lens around and sees things from a customer point of view. In each case, the fidelity/convenience trade-offs from "before" and "after" the inflection point would look very different.

The inflection point for cameras started with Philippe Kahn, a burly, bull-headed French jazz flutist who had come to America in the 1980s. He made a fortune founding Borland, one of the early personal computer software companies. He also made a habit of publicly feuding with Microsoft's Bill Gates, generally coming out on the losing end. In 1995, Kahn got pushed out of Borland in a dispute about the company's direction. Recognizing that cell phones were becoming smaller, more powerful, and more of a mass-market product, Kahn next founded a company called Starfish to design software for cell phones.

By 1997 the idea of a cell-phone camera seemed to be in the air. Putting the two together seemed—at least to forward-thinking engineers—as natural as putting butter on toast. In a sense, the problem was that nobody had invented the knife—the technology that could actually join the two in a convenient, workable way. That's where Kahn came in. He and his wife, Sonia Lee, arrived at the hospital in 1997 to give birth to their first child. Lee was going into labor, and Kahn, like a good husband, was at her side. "I'd gone to the Lamaze classes," Kahn told me. "And the second time I said, 'Breathe!' Sonia said, 'Shut up!' So I said, 'Okay, I'll sit at this desk and find something to do.'"

Kahn, a true tech geek, had come to the hospital outfitted with his laptop, cell phone, and digital camera. At the time, sharing digital photos meant taking a picture with a digital camera, downloading the shot to a laptop, connecting to the Internet, posting the photo to a website, and then e-mailing friends to tell them where to look. Kahn wanted to snap a picture, hit a button, and have the photo automatically load to the Web. As his wife's labor went on, Kahn, keeping quiet in his corner, fiddled with his hardware and wrote code to glue it together. "I had time to make a couple of trips to RadioShack to get soldering wire," he recalled. "I just stayed in the room and made that thing work." By the time he was holding his newborn daughter, Kahn could use his rigged-up contraption to take a digital photo and wirelessly post it for his friends and family.

Soon afterward, Motorola bought Starfish, Kahn's company. Kahn tried to persuade Motorola to adopt his camera-phone idea, but Motorola—which invented the cell phone—didn't see the potential. So Kahn formed a new company, LightSurf, to build and market PictureMail. It's a back-end system that lets a user take a photo with a cell phone camera and send it somewhere with a click or two. It is, so to speak, the knife in this story. The first version of PictureMail came out in Japan in 1999, and it spurred Japanese companies Sharp and Kyocera to make the first commercial camera phones. Nokia and other handset makers came later to the game. Kodak didn't get into making cell-phone cameras in a real way until 2008—in a partnership with Motorola.

In 2002, about 80 million camera phones were sold worldwide. By 2004, that number hit 233 million. In 2010, nearly 1 billion camera phones will be sold, according to InfoTrends/CAP Ventures.

The cell-phone camera has changed the way people think about photos. There used to be one kind of photo—the photos where you very purposefully took out a camera and took pictures. After camera phones, there were two types of photos: the convenient photos (little moments, shot with a camera phone because it was in your pocket, not intended to be printed or framed) and fidelity photos (significant moments, shot with a digital or film camera, with some hope that a good shot could be a lasting, displayable image). Thanks in large part to Kahn's invention, cell-phone cameras were a convenience revolution—a once-in-a-blue-moon meteor that shook up everything. Because so many people already carried a cell phone all the time, the camera phone became the first camera that was carried around by millions of people *all the time*. It is the most convenient system ever created for capturing images of daily life. Photos have never been so easy to take and share.

The fidelity/convenience equation for the picture-taking industry had, by the early 2000s, gone through a lot of changes because of digital cameras—but nothing like this. This was a seismic shift. In the 1980s, high-fidelity picture-taking would've involved a top-flight film camera with expensive lenses; the high-convenience version would've been a cheap Instamatic camera. When digital cameras came along, people still thought of picture-taking trade-offs much as they always had. There was high-fidelity picture-taking with expensive, high-megapixel digital cameras with expensive lenses, and high-convenience picture-taking, with cheaper, low-megapixel digital cameras you could buy at Target.

Cell-phone cameras wrecked that fidelity/convenience mindset, and created a new one. The new set of trade-offs involved different kinds of picture-taking—not just different kinds of stand-alone cameras. Now there is a market for purposeful, high-fidelity picture-taking, and there is a market for high-convenience picture-taking of daily moments. They are really two different markets.

Daily-moments picture-taking essentially didn't exist before the late 1990s. By the late 2000s, it overtook purposeful picture-taking. Nokia became the world's biggest maker of cameras—even though it has never made a stand-alone camera. According to InfoTrends, by 2010 the number of images captured on camera phones will reach 228 billion, exceeding the number taken on stand alone digital and film cameras combined. The camera industry got slammed by a wrecking-ball moment it never saw coming. Camera phones were such an extreme revolution in convenience that the old quality/convenience formula just couldn't support it. The new invention blew it apart.

What might this say about the picture-taking business? Well, if you're making cell-phone cameras, trying to package a cell phone with a beautiful camera marketed at purposeful, high-fidelity picture taking is probably not a great idea. These are two entirely different markets. People who are likely to put a camera on a tripod probably don't want their cell phone on a tripod. They'll buy a stand-alone digital camera instead.

/ / /

There is one other significant phenomenon that can affect the fidelity/convenience swap: products or services that become part of people's social lives can act as a fidelity turbocharger.

Bowling has long thrived because of social turbochargers. On the surface, bowling is a mid-fidelity, mid-convenience sport. It's not much of a glamorous sport, so it doesn't confer a whole lot of aura or identity on people who go to the bowling alley. Nor is it convenient. Bowling is relatively inexpensive, but you have to schlep somewhere to do it. But bowling is a highly social sport. It's a reason bowling alleys serve beer and pizza. Bowling leagues often become a center of participants' social lives. People who bowl pay money to the bowling alley as much to enjoy the social aspect as to bowl. The social aspect vastly boosts the experience—and thus the fidelity—of bowling.

Likewise, an "in" bar has a social factor that boosts its fidelity beyond that of a mere place that serves drinks. The board game Trivial Pursuit took off in the 1980s thanks to its social appeal. MySpace and Facebook are personal Web home pages with a social factor built in. In fact, MySpace and Facebook have made other companies aware of the power of online social systems as never before. For the first time, companies consciously plot how to inject a social aspect into products or services to gain an advantage.

Few people have thought longer about this than Trip Hawkins, who founded the video-game giant Electronic Arts in 1982. He eventually left the company to start 3DO and then, in 2003, a company called Digital Chocolate, which makes games and applications for cell phones—all based entirely on the concept of the social factor.

To Hawkins, it's obvious why companies like Nokia and Verizon Wireless tried and failed for years to get cell-phone games and video to take off. They just didn't get the social aspect of such games. Games and video on tiny cell-phone screens don't have much fidelity. And if they are meant to be played or viewed alone, they are unlikely to take off. "I am constantly pointing out that the [wireless] industry fixation on music and video, and on porting console video games to cell phones, and on making games based on films—it's all entirely misguided," Hawkins told me. "Mobile is not about fidelity. It's about social value."

Over the years, I talked with Hawkins a number of times about his philosophy of technology, and why certain things succeed and fail. Some of his ideas have influenced my thinking about the fidelity/convenience trade-off. Hawkins has always seemed like a different breed from many of the tech entrepreneurs I've met. He's an uber-geek trapped in a movie star's body—tanned, trim, perfectly coiffed and impeccably dressed, but underneath, still an awkward teenage programming whiz. At an industry conference before he gave a keynote talk, Hawkins confessed that he started Electronic Arts out of a sense of being a social outcast. "As a kid, I wanted people to play board games with me, but they wanted to watch TV," he said. "I thought, 'If I make games more like TV, people will play with me.'" It was the beginning of his thinking about social factors.

At Electronic Arts, one of his biggest hits was *Madden NFL*, a graphics-intensive, high-fidelity football video game. But while EA sold millions of the games, the total number of *Madden* players never came close to the total number of people playing fantasy football—a game based on statistics rather than on visual action. In fantasy football, a group of friends form a league, and each person builds a fantasy team by "drafting" various real NFL players. Winners and losers in the fantasy league are determined by the statistics the real players compile in the actual games. Fantasy football is extremely low-fidelity—except for the social aspect of friends playing against each other, and talking endlessly about the league. Similarly, Hawkins watched YouTube take off despite the generally horrible fidelity of its videos. YouTube's breakthrough was that for the first time it made uploading and viewing video on the Web very convenient. But YouTube really caught fire because of the way the site made it easy to share videos with friends. That was the social aspect of YouTube.

Hawkins kept watching cell-phone providers and content

owners trying to drive entertainment and games made for television screens onto cell-phone screens. They experimented with TV shows, sports clips, network news, and movies. Nokia made a combination cell phone and portable video-game unit called the N-Gage, which didn't catch on. "A lot of conventional content was trying to go mobile for five years, and it still added up to just two percent of mobile revenue," Hawkins said. "Ninety-eight percent of revenue was about communication. That tells you something." Cell phones, Hawkins concluded, are social devices. Their greatest value is in connecting people, not in delivering and playing content. Cell phones—even hot new phones like Apple's iPhone—have relatively small screens and tinny sound. Hawkins thought, *Why force content onto a platform that's not suited for it?* Instead, why not make content that takes advantage of what cell phones are all about?

Hawkins started Digital Chocolate to try a new approach to mobile games: make them low-fidelity, easy to use, and all about being social. In 2005 the company made a splash with a couple of social games. One was called *MLSN Sports Picks* (MLSN stands for Mobile League Sports Network). It was something of an online game show about sports. Users could create a league with a group of friends, who would all play at different times on their cell phones anywhere in the world. The other game was *AvaPeeps*. It let users create characters that go out on the network and try to date characters created by other people. Depending on their success, characters climb popularity rankings. Neither game tried to use all of a cell phone's processing power. The graphics were minimal. The allure was in the social connection, Hawkins said, not the on-screen experience.

While the games didn't set the universe on fire, they became popular enough to put Digital Chocolate on the mobile game industry's radar and prove Hawkins's point. AvaPeeps drove 400 messages a month per user, showing that the game deeply engaged those who played it. "Media companies tend to view content as being all about fidelity, and that's obsolete," Hawkins said. "Lower fidelity and social networks beats high fidelity. People don't even think they're spending money on content—they pay to improve their social value."

By 2007, few business executives had to be convinced that there was something to the social aspect of a product. MySpace and then Facebook became two of the most closely watched companies in the world—not just because they lured tens of millions of users, but because they became so important to users that they visited the sites frequently. Suddenly, every company wanted to build social networking into their products or services.

In 2006, when I was at *USA Today,* the newspaper's website drew up elaborate plans to try to add a social factor. It would allow readers to find each other, leave comments, interact—all with the idea that people would make friends inside of the *USA Today* site much the way bowling league participants make friends at a bowling alley. This would keep people coming back to the site and make it "stickier," the thinking went. But as of 2008, the social aspects of USATODAY.com didn't seem to be having much effect. The problem might have been that people have never particularly formed social groups around the newspapers they read. It seems to be difficult to add a social aspect to something that is not inherently social.

A company called LifeAt basically markets itself as a social site for apartment buildings. LifeAt builds a Facebook-like social networking website for a particular building or complex. Everyone who lives there can put up a profile and see the profiles of other residents. The guy who just moved into 5A and wishes he knew someone who played tennis might find that a woman in 8D is an avid tennis player and arrange an outing to the courts. If people in a building get to know one another and develop a social life around their neighbors, they'll be happier and might tend to stay longer.

Rap star 50 Cent has had a good deal of success adding a social aspect to his basic offering of hip-hop songs. In 2008 he created a website—ThisIs50.com—with built-in social networking capabilities. People tend to socialize around music artists. Teenagers who share a love of a particular artist listen to that artist together, go to a concert with a group, and talk about the music with each other. In the past decade, it's become common for just about every artist to put up an informational website. 50 Cent went a step further and built a site with the usual songs, biography, news, and videos—and social networking. Fans could meet one another through the site, talk about 50's music, and perhaps initiate online friendships. By mid-2008, the site had more than 100,000 members, and generated more buzz for 50 Cent than perhaps any artist's website before. The social aspect helped propel the site to unusual heights.

This would not surprise Hawkins. Social networking is the center of his business belief system. "Money is increasingly going to social value," he said. "Traditional media companies have not thought it out, but social media is the future."

PART TWO

Winners and Losers

CHAPTER FIVE

Super-Fidelity

Corning, the glass company, has thrived on high fidelity for 150 years.

Corning is based in and was named after Corning, New York, a picturesque and relatively wealthy village about four hours by car from New York City, surrounded by lakes, tree-covered hills, and farms. It's an interesting place to be the CEO of a $6-billion global corporation. "You go to the store, you see folks whose lives you're impacting," Corning CEO Wendell Weeks explained to me. "I don't have any secrets from the people of Corning. Every traffic ticket I've ever gotten, I'm sure they know."

The small-town atmosphere plays a role in how Corning acts as a company. There's something dynastic yet homespun about the corporate culture. "I came into adulthood working in an institution where values matter, where people matter, where what you do matters not only for today but for the generations that follow," Weeks says. "You're part of this long line that goes back 150-plus years. It makes you think about how you will set up the person who follows you. The unique thing about our company is we think that way."

Weeks has spent his entire career at Corning. Tall, lanky, easygoing, with a dry, sharp sense of humor, Weeks is responsible for taking Corning to its greatest heights—and, bizarrely, for playing a major role in its near death. In the 1990s, Weeks, not yet forty, ran Corning's fiberoptic business. The company invented optical fiber and made much of the fiber that telecommunications companies around the world used to build their high-speed networks. By the late 1990s, telecom companies were booming, buying everything Corning could churn out. Corning came to rely on that business like an addict. Fiber made up 80 percent of the company's profits. Weeks built factories and added employees, committing even more of Corning's resources to its fiberoptics habit. At the peak of telecom mania, Corning was worth $120 billion.

Then the unexpected happened. The telecom industry crashed. Scandals at Enron, Worldcom, and Global Crossing shut down major fiber projects. A slowing economy cut the growth in data traffic traveling over fiber, making the building of new networks temporarily unnecessary. Orders for fiber were canceled seemingly overnight. The mess nearly brought down Weeks's division and the whole of Corning with it. In 2002 the company's worth fell to $1.5 billion, its stock price barely above $1. "The institution was under assault," Weeks said.

A lot of companies might have fired Weeks for his miscalculations about the fiber market. Instead, Corning CEO Jamie Houghton, who was ready to retire, promoted Weeks from his job running the fiber division to CEO. "To paraphrase slightly, Jamie said, 'You helped screw this up. You help fix it,'" Weeks said. He added sarcastically, "That's a slight paraphrase." Houghton did not use the word "screw."

Weeks felt confident that Corning could be fixed, but not by radically changing the company. He'd fix it by turning back to what Corning did best. "A crisis is too good an opportunity to waste," Weeks said. "We used the opportunity to decide what type of company we were going to be. We embraced the core of what we do—which is to create and make keystone components and grow through innovation."

And there is the secret to what Corning has done over and over for 150 years. It invests huge sums of money in decade-long research projects to produce wildly advanced glass-based products that no competitor can match. Corning rarely tries to make a product for consumers—though in the past it made dishes and coffeepots. More typically, it makes glass products that are used in making something else, becoming a key—or keystone, in Weeks's language—component in a brand-new high-tech product or system. In the 1800s, Corning made highly specialized glass for Thomas Edison's first lightbulbs. The company invented and manufactured the glass that made color TVs possible. It invented the optical fiber that now carries just about all the world's data and voice traffic. Corning invented and makes the glass that is going into most of the world's flat-screen TVs. Flat-screen TVs became a wildly successful business for Corning. "We lost money on that for fourteen years before it became the overnight success that it is right now," Weeks told me in 2007.

Corning is the world's highest-fidelity glass technology company. The company invests in new high-fidelity products, leaping years ahead of its competitors, and charging premium prices.

Thanks to refocusing on fidelity, Corning has not just turned itself around—it's in a better position now than when fiberoptics was red hot. The company may never have the inflated market capitalization that it had in the late 1990s, but that was crazy valuation in a crazy era. In mid-2008, Corning was worth $32 billion—almost twenty times the $1.5 billion it was valued at in 2002. Corning has a number of growing, profitable, high-fidelity product lines, and more in the pipeline, while its scientists work on ideas for the next decade.

/ / /

In any market segment, there's usually at least one high-fidelity player that every other player admires and strives to imitate. That entity does things better than everyone else. People love the product or service. They want to own it, to make it part of their identity. They will tolerate terrible inconveniences—high prices, difficulty in obtaining it—to acquire it. Like some strange law of quantum physics, at the pinnacle of fidelity, convenience can almost disappear. Instead, pure desire takes over. Even lust.

Apple got there with the first iPhones. Years before that, one could've found Motorola at the pinnacle of fidelity with its RAZR—which cost consumers more than $400 at a time when many other cell phones came free with a service contract. Singapore Airlines' first-class cabin is the pinnacle of fidelity in air travel; Louis Vuitton, in handbags. Whole Foods in the 2000s became the high-fidelity choice of grocery stores. There are always restaurants—sometimes for a short time and sometimes for decades—that offer the highest-fidelity experience. One example is The French Laundry in California's Napa Valley. (Talk about inconvenience—dinner costs $300 per person without wine, and you have to speed-dial the reservation line two months in advance to get a table.) On a grander scale, the U.S. armed forces are the highest-fidelity of militaries—admired and unbe-lievably inconvenient considering an annual defense budget of some $440 billion.

Being the highest-fidelity company or having the highest-fidelity product or service is a great place to be. Cirque du Soleil, for example, has created an all-senses-engaged entertainment experience that simply can't be duplicated by any other means. It charges $100 or more for tickets and sells out nearly every show—no small feat in an age of 3-D movies, realistic computer games, and myriad other forms of entertainment. The company brought in $700 million in revenue in 2007, and is worth around $2 billion. No "normal" circus company could approach that level of success.

Bose, the music speaker company, created a high-fidelity hit with the Bose QuietComfort headphones. High-end headphones have been around for decades. And headphones based on noise-canceling technology—which generates sound waves inside the unit that interfere with and cancel out the kind of droning noise you get on an airliner—have been available since the 1990s. Bose put those concepts together and went for the very top end of the market. The QuietComfort headphones, first out in 2000, used Bose speaker technology, which already had a top-shelf reputa-tion, and added the best noise-canceling technology the company could pack into a headset. The result was a set of headphones that cost $300 and were far bulkier and harder to carry on a plane than typical iPhone earbuds.

Crazy, right? Totally inconvenient. Who would spend as much on the headphones as you'd spend on an iPod? As it turned out, business travelers who fly all the time were happy to shell out $300 for a gadget that would not only make music and movies sound better in flight, but would ultimately save their hearing. As high-mileage travelers started wearing them, the QuietComfort phones became a status symbol on flights. The bulky, unique shape actually worked in Bose's favor: if you wore QuietComfort headphones, everyone *knew* you were wearing them. That only added to the phones' fidelity—because the product gained an aura and became a way for business travelers to identify themselves as hard-core, savvy, well-to-do fliers. That, in turn, made more people aspire to buy QuietComfort headphones. Sony, Philips, and other companies later came out with expensive noise-canceling headphones, but none acquired the cachet of Bose's headphones.

High fidelity can help a new kind of product break through in the marketplace. Companies have tried to break through with electric cars for decades. General Motors took a run at making an electric car for the mass market in the 1990s. It was canned by 2003. All electric cars suffered from the same problem: they were inconvenient *and* low-fidelity. They were inconvenient primarily because they couldn't travel far enough without needing to be recharged. So consumers wouldn't consider purchasing an electric car as a primary vehicle. Electric cars were low-fidelity because every company thought an electric car should be small and utilitarian, on top of having a fraction of the performance of a gas-powered car. So nobody thought of an electric car as a great car. In the fidelity/convenience equation, electric cars were perennially stuck deep in the fidelity belly—and consumers predictably responded with apathy. The general public may like the idea of electric cars that can help save the environment, but the models that came out gave consumers few reasons to either love or need one, much less buy one.

In the 2000s, Martin Eberhard and Elon Musk approached electric cars from a different direction. Eberhard had started and sold a few tech companies, including the electronic book company NuvoMedia, which he sold for $187 million. He noticed that a lot of people who owned a Prius also owned a Porsche or some other sports car. He realized the Prius was more of a statement about the environment for those people than a real, daily transportation solution. His epiphany was that he should make a car that combined the two: a high-fidelity sports car that made an environmental statement.[1]

Eberhard got an initial $6.3-million investment from Musk, who'd made hundreds of millions of dollars selling the company he'd cofounded, PayPal, to eBay. In 2004 the two started Tesla Motors—and feuded relentlessly over the next four years. The company operated in Silicon Valley, far outside of the traditional auto industry home of Detroit. By 2008 the first model, dubbed the Tesla Roadster, was ready to market. It looked like a classic, super-hot sports car—and drove like no other sports car, ever. Hit the accelerator—one can't really call it a "gas pedal" on the Tesla—and the car would rocket from zero to sixty miles per hour in 3.9 seconds. The G forces literally could push the driver's head back against the headrest. And its electric motor was almost silent. The Roadster took 3.5 hours to charge, and could travel 220 miles before recharging. Its base price: $109,000.

Though only the wealthy could afford Tesla Roadsters (on the waiting list in 2008: George Clooney, Arnold Schwarzenegger, Google cofounder Larry Page), the Roadster may well go down in history as the car that made electric cars a successful consumer product. By aiming for super-fidelity—essentially aiming at making the hottest sports car on the market, whether gas or electric—Tesla attempted to bust electric cars out of the fidelity belly. The Tesla Roadster's performance won the car so much media attention that the car took on a special aura. Owning one is a statement—less about the environment, and more about the owner's personal success and savvy. Want to get noticed? Rocket from a Hollywood Hills party without making a sound.

Next, Tesla plans to make a $60,000 family sedan. And now General Motors has revived plans for electric cars. The Tesla Roadster may or may not be a successful product in the long run, but it has made people believe that electric cars can be performance vehicles, rather than just compromise vehicles loved only by environmentalists. That change in thinking could only happen with the arrival of a very high-fidelity product.

/ / /

Although achieving the highest fidelity is a great niche to occupy in a category, maintaining that position can be difficult. Technology is constantly pushing out the edges of fidelity—constantly making it possible to create even higher fidelity. Any high-fidelity product or service will run into trouble if it sits still. Another company will inevitably come along and make a competing product or service with even higher fidelity.

Motorola's RAZR is an example. In early 2003, a team of Motorola engineers and designers started with a mock-up of a super-slim phone, and worked backward to invent the technology to make it possible. "I'll never forget the day Ralph Pini [who led the team] pulled a crummy aluminum prototype out of his shirt pocket with two fingers and said, 'We ought to make this,'" Daniel Nickel, a former Motorola executive, told me. One of the team's managers told me it took six months to convince top management the RAZR could be a viable product.[2]

When, in early 2004, incoming Motorola CEO Ed Zander showed prototypes to major wireless carriers, they didn't like it and thought it was too expensive. The phone had a revolutionary, sleek, fashionable design, and would retail for more than $400. Zander and Geoffrey Frost—a former Nike marketer whom Motorola had hired—believed Motorola could make the phones seem so cool that consumers would want them despite the price. Whether they knew it or not, they were operating on the basis of fidelity—making something that leaped to the top of fidelity in the cell-phone market.

In the fall of 2004, Motorola unveiled the phone. In the fourth quarter that year, Motorola shipped 750,000 RAZRs—not many, considering that Motorola shipped a total of 29 million handsets that quarter. Motorola planned to make 2 million RAZRs in 2005. But the head of the cell-phone division, Ron Garriques, pushed for 20 million, and the phone took off. In 2005 the company shipped 146 million phones, up 40 percent over 2004, and most of the growth came from the RAZR.

But the RAZR masked what was otherwise *not* happening in the cell-phone division. Resources and attention all went to that one success. Little was done to follow it up with new and better inventions. Motorola missed the next shift in cell-phone technology. RAZR and its ilk were all 2G phones—built on networks like AT&T's Edge. But by 2006 the hottest phones ran on 3G networks that were faster and built for data and video as well as voice calls.

RAZR, once the super-fidelity phone, started slipping off that summit. Motorola watched as competitors made phones of higher fidelity. And then Motorola made a huge mistake. With competitors surging into 3G, Motorola decided to slash prices on the RAZR and go for volume and market share. In other words, it shifted strategy and went after convenience. At first it seemed to work. RAZRs saturated the market. Motorola sold more than 100 million—making RAZR by far the most popular cell phone in history.

But it also destroyed the RAZR brand. Consumers who once considered the RAZR the high-fidelity phone now saw it as the cheap phone you get when signing a wireless contract. The RAZR lost both its technological edge and its aura, and that destroyed the RAZR's high-fidelity position. Motorola had relied so much on the RAZR, it didn't have a new high-fidelity product to replace it. So Motorola lost its positioning and became a maker of phones that fell smack into the fidelity belly, with so-so fidelity and so-so convenience.

As a result, Motorola's financial performance fell off a cliff in 2006. Near the end of 2007 the company pushed out CEO Zander. Motorola's inability to keep up with the cell-phone market cost the company dearly.

/ / /

I grew up in Binghamton, New York, about a mile from an impressive stone mansion that belonged to one of the pioneers of *perceived* fidelity—which today is a powerful force behind beer commercials, designer clothes, and a range of other high-end products. Willis Sharpe Kilmer was one of the earliest modern businessmen to aim for high fidelity based almost entirely on aura. The product he marketed was something few readers of this book probably ever heard of: a patent medicine called Swamp-Root. It was one of the most successful patent medicines of all time. Its story illustrates both the power and fragility of perceived fidelity.

In the late 1800s, Andral Kilmer was a popular physician in and around Binghamton. He practiced both homeopathic medicine and more-traditional medicine—his studies ranged from course work at the Eclectic and Botanic Practice in Wisconsin to Bellevue Hospital and Medical College in New York. He concocted his own remedies for his patients, and by the 1870s Andral's brother, Jonas Kilmer, moved to Binghamton to help run a small factory to make them. The medicines included Dr. Kilmer's Ocean Weed Heart Remedy; Female Remedy; and Dr. Kilmer's Swamp-Root Kidney, Liver and Bladder Cure. Swamp-Root, as you might imagine, didn't actually cure anything. It contained more than a dozen natural extracts that together acted as a diuretic, making people urinate a lot so they thought their kidneys and urinary tract were functioning better. The 10 percent alcohol content didn't hurt the potion's appeal, either.

Jonas Kilmer's son, Willis Kilmer, graduated from Cornell University in 1880, and his father brought the young man into the family business, making him head of the advertising department. The timing coincided with the emergence of mass-market advertising for all kinds of health and personal hygiene products, like soap and aspirin.[3] Willis Kilmer took the trend to a new level. He touted the virtues of Swamp-Root—the most successful of his uncle's recipes—on billboards, posters, and circulars, and in newspaper ads. He created the *Swamp-Root Almanac*—an annual thirty-page color pamphlet that alternated horoscopes, dream interpretation guides, and weather forecasts with page after page of information about the importance of kidney care and testimonials about Swamp-Root's effectiveness. The almanacs were essentially an 1880s version of the infomercial.

All in all, Swamp-Root came to be seen as something special. People around the world believed it rejuvenated their kidneys and kept them healthier. It was complete hype—100 percent aura. Of the hundreds of medical cures on the market, Swamp-Root broke through with a high-fidelity image. Dr. Kilmer & Co. became a global operation, marketing Swamp-Root in Europe and South America. No one can be sure how many bottles were sold, but the Kilmers piled up one of the biggest fortunes in southern New York. (When asked what Swamp-Root was good for, Willis supposedly answered, "About a million dollars a year.") Willis Kilmer built a mansion, started a newspaper, and owned a racehorse operation that produced the 1918 Kentucky Derby winner, Exterminator.

Around 1900, Dr. Kilmer & Co. was more successful and certainly better known than two other medicine companies active at the time, Merck and Johnson & Johnson. So why isn't Kilmer & Co. a modern-day Merck or J&J? Around 1900, journalists and activists started exposing dangerous foods and misleading labeling, culminating in Congress passing the Pure Food and Drug Act of 1906.[4] The debate and the new law, which forced companies to accurately label food and medicines, introduced skepticism about patent medicines in general—Swamp-Root among them. Because Swamp-Root was built on nothing but aura, once that bubble burst, its high-fidelity status went with it. The Swamp-Root business lived on for decades. I have a *Swamp-Root Almanac* dated 1935. But it fell into the fidelity belly, and went from a fortune-making phenomenon into a mediocre, slowly deflating business. After World War II, the family sold out to Medtech Laboratories of Wyoming.

Trying to push a product to high fidelity on aura is a strategy that has never gone out of fashion. Beer has always relied on aura for its popularity. Take the beer Yuengling. Yuengling has been made in Pottsville, Pennsylvania, since 1829. In the 1980s it was considered a low-class, inexpensive local beer available in Pennsylvania and New York State. In 1985, Richard Yuengling Jr.—a new generation of the founding family—took charge, increased manufacturing capacity, and started making Yuengling more widely available. The brand caught on as a mid-priced, microbrew favorite, and by the mid-2000s Yuengling had become the sixth-biggest U.S. brewer. It was all based on aura. No doubt most people who order a Yuengling in a bar couldn't identify it in a blind taste test against any of dozens of other similar beers. But it became socially intriguing—even cool—to order Yuengling. Contrast that to a beer like Schlitz. In 1970, Schlitz had 12.1 percent of the U.S. beer market.[5] By 1990 the brand had all but disappeared. Same beer, completely different aura. Order Schlitz in a bar, and your friends would most likely poke fun at you.

Crocs—essentially colorful plastic gardening clogs that by all rights should never have had more fashion cachet than galoshes—are another example of a product that somehow took hold and acquired an aura of hipness, climbing high up the fidelity side of the casual-shoe sector. Consumers were willing to pay twenty-five to seventy dollars for Crocs, even though similar plastic clogs could be found in Wal-Mart for five dollars. It was a classic case of fidelity over convenience. In 2007, Crocs Inc. had $847 million in sales.[6]

But by 2008, Crocs had become so commonplace that any

sense of identity conferred upon their owners disappeared, which took Crocs' aura with it. *Newsweek* poked fun at the shoes, saying they were only worn by "dorks." Sales took a dive, and so did the stock price, and in mid-2008 the company started laying off workers. Everyone noticed that the emperor had no clothes—the ultimate threat for any product or service built on aura.

/ / /

Is super-fidelity sustainable?

Corning shows that it is. But sustainability requires constant investment and long-term thinking. It helps if the fidelity of a product results from a real, tangible competitive advantage. As the stories of Swamp-Root and Crocs suggest, the more a product or service relies on aura alone, the more susceptible that product is to getting toppled from its perch.

Perhaps no one in business understands fidelity better than casino owner Steve Wynn. His father ran a string of bingo parlors in the Northeast. Steve took over the family operation and leveraged it to buy a small stake in the Frontier Hotel and Casino in Las Vegas in the 1960s. He eventually bought controlling interest in the Golden Nugget, renovating it from a shabby casino into a resort. In the 1980s he spent $630 million building the Mirage on Las Vegas's strip, and its size and luxuriousness topped anything in the city at the time. Wynn next constructed Treasure Island on the Strip, and then the $1.6-billion Bellagio. In the 2000s, he topped them all by building the Wynn for $2.7 billion.

At each step, Wynn built a hotel and casino that topped his competitors not by just a little, but by a huge margin—and put him in the super-fidelity position. Each time, other developers followed by matching or going just beyond Wynn's standard. It was the tech effect writ large. And each time, Wynn responded with a project that leaped far beyond competing properties and reclaimed the super-fidelity position. Of course, each response was a costly, risky bet. He kept reaching out to do something no one had done before. But that's the key to super-fidelity, and the approach seems to be part of Wynn's very fiber.

"I remember when he was describing the Mirage to me," said Bobby Kotick, the CEO of Activision, who has been like an adopted son to Wynn. When I interviewed Kotick at his Beverly Hills home, the conversation kept turning back to Wynn. "He didn't even own the dirt yet. But he would describe the bronze inlay in the floors or the fish tank that would be behind the check-in, and it would turn out exactly as he envisioned it. He would come up with these creative concepts in his mind, and he could execute them. And always, he was thinking about how he was going to be the highest-margin operator, how he was going to be the most profitable operator."

Wynn told an interviewer on ABC's *Nightline* in 2007, "It's about the non-casino parts. People don't move for a slot machine. What moves people is the notion that when they have time for recreation and leisure, they can go somewhere and have an experience that's richer, more exciting, maybe more beautiful or fun than they can get every other day." Or, he could have added, at any other property.[7]

Wynn's natural drive toward fidelity is so big it's affected not just his business, but a whole city. Because of hotels like the Mirage, the Bellagio, and the Wynn, Las Vegas became a high-fidelity destination city—the kind of place so sensational it can't be duplicated anywhere else. You can go lots of places to gamble. You can go lots of places to stay in a luxury hotel. But nothing matches the total experience of Las Vegas.

"Having been along for the ride, and being that close to watching someone change a city, it sets the bar so high for any kind of accomplishment," said Kotick. "I think that actually drove me to even be more successful."

Achieving the highest level of fidelity is hard. And if someone catches up, you have to invest and sweat until you come up with something that's far better yet.

CHAPTER SIX

Super-Convenience

In 1981, when I was in college at Rutgers, I visited a longtime friend, Deb, at Rensselaer Polytechnic Institute in Troy, New York. Deb was a serious, straight-A engineering student. But when I walked into her apartment, she was sitting joyously glued to this new thing on cable television called MTV. She couldn't stop watching, she told me. It was a revelation to her. For the first time, she could *see* the music she loved. Millions of others felt the same, and MTV, in a flash, became a cultural hurricane, changing the way music connected with fans and the way it was marketed. MTV even altered the kinds of artists who made it big. Looking "hot" became a massive strategic advantage, thanks to music videos.

So where did MTV go right? Did it win on the fidelity side or the convenience side? If looked at through the lens of "twenty-four-hour broadcast music," MTV was a fidelity victory over the only alternative at the time: radio. MTV added visuals to the music and made it a richer experience. That wasn't the approach MTV's founding programmer took, however. Instead, Bob Pittman believed that MTV was about "seeing pop stars perform their songs." Before MTV, you might catch a glimpse of a favorite artist on *American Bandstand* or *Soul Train* or a variety show. But those moments were scattered and hard to find on TV. In terms of "seeing pop stars perform their songs," Pittman realized, fans could choose the high-fidelity route of going to a concert. But that was not a high-convenience solution. MTV wasn't competing against radio, Pittman believed—it competed against the maddening difficulty of seeing artists play. Pittman decided to exploit that hole in the market. "MTV was born out of television getting convenient," Pittman told me.[1] "It was completely about convenience."

Pittman is the high-convenience yin to Steve Wynn's fidelity yang. In his three-decade career, Pittman made MTV into a phenomenon, helped AOL to explode on the Internet, and pumped up the businesses of such seemingly disparate entities as Century 21 Real Estate and Six Flags amusement parks. Unlikely as it might seem, Pittman sees a central idea running through all those ventures. "Everything I've done is about convenience," he told me. "Every business, no matter what it is—you find convenience over your competitors, and you win."

We talked in the office of his investment firm, Pilot Group, in Manhattan's Rockefeller Center. On a shelf by Pittman's desk stood a small statue of one of the famous MTV astronauts, a fashion-industry award (for the influence MTV had on fashion), and a plaque stating that the Jackson, Mississippi, native had been inducted into the Mississippi Business Hall of Fame. In his own way, Pittman has plotted his career on the basis of the fidelity/convenience trade-off, always looking for a way to jump to the far end of the convenience side of the spectrum.

In the 1980s, the proliferation of cable TV opened the way for twenty-four-hour niche networks like Cable News Network,

Home Box Office, and Music Television. This allowed viewers to watch the kind of programming they wanted, when they wanted. Instead of planning their schedules around, say, *The CBS Evening News*, viewers could turn on CNN anytime and get the news. For the music-loving market, MTV quickly proved the easiest, best, most convenient way to hear and *see* favorite artists.

Pittman had been something of a programming prodigy, starting as a disk jockey in Jackson when he was fifteen. At twenty-four, he was hired as a program director for WNBC-AM in New York. That led to a job in TV as the head of programming for Warner Amex, which wanted to develop a music channel. He made the channel—MTV—into an instant hit. When MTV started, it reached 6 million cable subscribers. Three years later, that was up to 25 million and growing.

In the late 1980s, Pittman was at Warner when it merged with Time. The new Time Warner owned Six Flags and made Pittman CEO of the unit. To hear Pittman tell it, he essentially constructed a theme park fidelity/convenience trade-off in his head. Disney's parks sat firmly in the highest-fidelity position, and there seemed to be no way to dislodge them. Disney was unbeatable in fidelity. So how could Six Flags compete? By focusing on high convenience, Pittman decided. Six Flags built parks in more locations, making them easier for more people to get to. And they didn't have the crowds, or the high prices, of Disney parks. "Our tagline was 'Bigger than Disneyland; closer to home,'" Pittman said. "We were not *better* than Disney, but we were more convenient. We went from 17 million visitors a year to 25 million by going after convenience."

A few years later, in 1995, Pittman took the CEO job at Century 21, a nationwide real estate brokerage network. Again, Pittman pushed the company in the direction of super-convenience by making Century 21 a "one-stop shop" for information, loans, moving plans, or anything else that went along with shopping for a house. This was just before the rise of the Web, when even something like getting basic information about schools in a given community could be difficult. Century 21 aimed to be the one real estate firm that could handle all home buyer needs. "Our strategy was all about convenience," said Pittman.

Next, America Online CEO Steve Case hired Pittman to be his Number 2. AOL had already become the world's largest on-line service by becoming the high-convenience player on the Internet. Compared to early online competitors like Compuserve and Prodigy, AOL made things so simple almost anyone could use it. Yet in the mid-1990s, AOL was growing so fast that it increasingly had service problems. And it kept adding features that threatened to make the service harder to navigate. The media were beating up on AOL, and customers began looking for alternatives. (AOL was needed, but, boy, it was not loved in those years.) Whether Case knew it or not, he hired exactly the right person at the right time—someone who would take AOL back to its high-convenience roots. "I used to fight with the engineers," Pittman told me. "I'd ask, 'Is it easier?' They'd say, 'No, it's better.' I'd say, 'But is it easier? If not, don't bother.' AOL had to be the most convenient. Convenience wins."

Pittman helped put AOL back on track. While Pittman was there, AOL grew from 6 million subscribers to 30 million. By 2000, AOL was so big and powerful that it merged with Time Warner in a deal worth, at the time, around $180 billion. That merger famously turned into a corporate catastrophe, and Pittman left to invest in startups through the Pilot Group. He's had a few hits among his portfolio of companies, including the fashion e-mail newsletter DailyCandy, the music social networking service iLike, and the online TV channel Next New Networks. In every case, he's aimed for high convenience. Any entrepreneur who comes through Pittman's door had better have a convenience pitch. "It's what I look for," Pittman says. "It's in my brain."

/ / /

High convenience is typically low margin, but huge volume. It is often ubiquitous. Convenience is not about creating a beautiful experience, or about aura or identity. Sometimes it doesn't offer a good experience at all, and doesn't do a thing to enhance one's identity. High convenience is not about love, but about need. At its best, it is about habit. And when a product or service becomes habit, it can be hard to dislodge.

McDonald's by the 1970s became the pinnacle of convenience in terms of eating out. The restaurants are everywhere, and they're cheap, fast, simple, familiar, well run, and clean, and they offer the easiest way to get a meal quickly away from home. Despite armies of fast-food competitors over the years, despite criticism, despite the fact that more people are likely to say they love their dentist than say they love McDonald's, McDonald's has not yet been pushed from its super-convenience position. For lack of a better way to put it, McDonald's is habit.

When Ford's Model T went into production in 1908, it became the world's first high-convenience car. It wasn't flashy; it only came in black. But Ford's innovative mass-production techniques allowed it to make the cars cheaply and pump them out in high volume—which meant the Model T was easy to find and relatively affordable for middle-class consumers.

Southland Corporation made its 7-Eleven stores into the high-convenience way to pick up badly needed supplies, driving independent corner grocers out of business.

Dupont in 1940 introduced nylon stockings, which became far more convenient than silk stockings. They actually cost more to buy up front, but far less in the long run (if you'll pardon the pun) because they lasted longer and were easier to care for. Nylons captured 30 percent of the hosiery market within two years after hitting store shelves.[2]

Yet chasing convenience can be tricky. In 1985, Yugo America began importing cars from the Yugoslavian automaker Zastava Koral. The Yugo was intended to be a high-convenience car. Its sticker price—$3,990—was by far the lowest of any car sold in the United States. The company set up ninety dealerships, and individuals put down deposits on the whole first shipment of 1,500 Yugos. But as consumers started driving the cars, they found that Yugos were not as convenient as they first appeared. The shoddy cars frequently broke down, and repair shops at Yugo dealerships developed a reputation for terrible service. In no time, the Yugo became the punchline to many jokes. (Why does a Yugo have a rear window defroster? To keep your hands warm as you push it. How do you double the value of a Yugo? Fill the tank with gas.) The sticker price may have been convenient, but owning a Yugo was highly inconvenient. And in 1992, Yugo America went out of business.[3]

Here is another high-convenience miss: In the late 1990s, well-funded dot-com startup Webvan decided to tackle the grocery store. Grocery stores had not become significantly more convenient in decades. Customers still had to drive to them, walk the aisles, fill a cart, stand in a checkout line, put the bags in the trunk, drive home, and then unload the bags. Webvan thought it could become the super-convenient grocery store by eliminating all those steps. It would let consumers order on the Web, and groceries would be delivered to their homes and piled right on their kitchen counters. Webvan planned to build a giant distribution center in every major city—a single facility that could take the place of dozens of traditional grocery stores. The idea sounded so compelling that by mid-1999, Webvan had attracted $120 million in funding from companies such as CBS, Knight-Ridder, and major venture capital firms.

But once Webvan was launched, consumers didn't find the service convenient enough. The majority of people weren't used to shopping online, especially for groceries. For them, getting set up with Webvan seemed daunting and took a lot of time. Customers often couldn't get the best delivery slots—such as in the evening after work. Once delivered, items such as fruit and deli meat sometimes weren't the right type or didn't have the quality the consumer would have looked for if he or she had been at the store in person. A lot of customers found that they still wound up going to the grocery store to get items they didn't want to buy from Webvan—which didn't exactly make customers' lives significantly easier. By 2000—six quarters after opening for business—Webvan's first distribution center in Oakland, California, was operating at only 30-percent capacity. Webvan's losses piled higher as the service failed to win enough new converts to cover the costs of such Goliath operations. In July 2001, the company closed its doors for good.[4]

Yugo tried to be super-convenient on price, and Webvan on the element of time. Both failed because they didn't realize that convenience is a more holistic package—you have to be good at everything that makes a product or service easy to get and use.

Nonetheless, the business landscape is full of companies

that became convenience winners, despite dimwitted executives who didn't always understand the innovation they had at their disposal.

ATMs seem as if they should have been a super-convenience no-brainer to banking executives. Today, ATMs are the easiest way to get cash. Remember when you had to go to a teller during banking hours? Carry traveler's checks on trips? Those are among the inconvenient services the ATM vanquished. But bankers originally couldn't see that. They thought they were in a fidelity business—offering a complex financial-social relationship, like George Bailey's savings and loan in *It's a Wonderful Life*. For most consumers, though, banks were in the business of safely holding their money until they needed it. That's it. There was no fidelity involved. No one felt proud that they did business with one bank over another. And one of the main things customers wanted from a bank was to be able to get money out quickly when they needed it. Customers wanted convenience.

Don Wetzel helped invent the automated teller machine at a little company called Docutel in the 1960s. The very idea of an ATM at the time seemed bizarre. Average folks didn't operate computers or smart, automated machinery. There were no PCs or VCRs or even electronic calculators back then. Telephones still had rotary dials. At work, most of the population didn't use anything more sophisticated than a typewriter. It was not obvious to banking executives that customers would trust a machine with something as important as their money.

Docutel met resistance from bankers, who mistakenly thought customers craved a high-fidelity relationship with tellers. "The bankers always said, 'Our customers, they know Susie, they've known her for a long time, and they feel very comfortable coming and talking to her, and Susie likes to talk to them,'"

Wetzel said in an interview with the National Museum of American History. "Neither was true. Susie didn't know the customer. I didn't know my teller. I didn't go to the same teller, especially if this line over there was shorter. I went over there and I couldn't have cared less who the teller was. So their thinking was not on target. Once we got past the hurdle of convincing [bankers] that people would use this machine because of the convenience factor, then we were able to move forward as fast as we could."

Even then, penetration took a while. The first ATM in the United States went into service at a Chemical Bank in New York in 1969. In 1973, 2,000 ATMs were in operation. The machines didn't take off until the 1980s, once it became obvious that many customers would rather use an ATM and never walk into a bank branch. By 1986, there were 64,000 ATMs installed.[5] Today, ATM machines are in banks, stores, gas stations, hotels, and schools in every corner of the world. There are ATMs in the Forbidden City in Beijing. ATMs have become one of history's great super-convenience inventions.

/ / /

One of the all-time kings of high convenience in the retail industry is Wal-Mart. But it learned a hard lesson about the risks of compromising its position in the fidelity/convenience trade-off.

Founder Sam Walton started Wal-Mart in rural markets, where consumers previously had to shop by driving to small, independent shops scattered around town or around the region. Those shops had little buying power or scale, so their prices were typically on the high side. If a shop—say, a hardware store— happened to be down the street, it was quite convenient. But on the whole, shopping for the necessities of life in a rural area took up a lot of time traveling to stores that had high prices and not much selection.

Wal-Mart would come to town and build a gigantic super-store. A Wal-Mart would offer more goods than dozens of independent shops within miles. As Wal-Mart gained scale, it gained buying power, and forced prices lower. Walton started Wal-Mart in 1962 with the intention of becoming the low-price retailer. Yet Wal-Mart didn't win just by offering low prices. Wal-Mart won because, especially in rural areas, it offered by far the easiest way to buy all of life's necessities. Price was one part of that. But the other part was making shopping easier for rural and suburban consumers. In 1980, Wal-Mart had 330 stores. By 1990 it had more than 1,500. By the mid-2000s, it had more than 7,000 facilities around the world and more than $300 billion in annual sales.

But in about 2000, Wal-Mart seemed to develop a corporate brain freeze. It started doing things that were out of step with its long heritage in super-convenience. For one, it tried to push into the center of major cities like New York and Chicago. In Manhattan, for instance, there are hundreds of shops within a few blocks of nearly everyone. Traveling halfway across town to get to a Wal-Mart superstore might actually be more inconvenient than finding the same products in nearby shops. Wal-Mart loses some of its convenience advantage in cities. City dwellers just don't seem to care whether Wal-Mart comes in or not. In fact, New Yorkers fought *against* the company. Exasperated, CEO Lee Scott told the *New York Times*, "I don't think it's worth the effort."[6] In 2007, Wal-Mart gave up on New York. In fact, Wal-Mart should never have tried, if it wanted to stay true to its core principles.

Around the same time, Wal-Mart started carrying higher-priced, more fashionable clothes. It tried advertising in upscale magazines like *Vogue*. Wal-Mart seemed to be forgetting its roots as the lowest-cost retailer; it seemed determined to develop aura. But consumers weren't interested. They just wanted stuff cheap.

Sure enough, the company's growth stalled and its stock price dipped. Wal-Mart's stock slipped from sixty dollars a share in 2004 to forty-three dollars a share in late 2007. So Wal-Mart pulled back on its urban plans, got rid of the fashion ads and pricier clothes, and launched a new ad campaign around the slogan: "Save money. Live better."[7] The campaign reconfirmed Wal-Mart's position as a retailer of super-convenience. And customers came back—helped along by a sagging economy that made low prices attractive to more people. Sales rebounded, and by the summer of 2008, Wal-Mart's stock was back to sixty dollars.

/ / /

Achieving high convenience can be a long slog. It doesn't happen quickly. It seems possible to offer a high-fidelity product or service right out of the box, as Tesla Motors did with its Roadster. High convenience, though, means attracting mass markets, which means selling on a big scale. Webvan tried to create scale right from the start; but it cost so much money to do that, when customers didn't come along right away, the company folded under the weight of its operations. Sam Walton started with one store and grew slowly.

When Sky Dayton started EarthLink in 1994, he was focused on the concept of convenience. Dayton was not a technologist— he was just a precocious young businessman. In 1990, at age nineteen, he'd opened an art gallery and coffee shop in Los Angeles, called Café Mocha. It caught on, and the place soon had lines down the block. A few years later, Dayton heard about the

Internet, which was just getting under way. Dayton recalls spending eighty hours trying to get connected, and feeling extremely frustrated. He felt he could offer something better. And that's when he decided to start EarthLink.

"EarthLink wasn't the only Internet provider," Dayton told me as I interviewed him in front of an audience at UCLA's business school. "In fact, we had in L.A., within six months of starting, easily one hundred competitors. And we just did it better."

Dayton pulled out his original business plan—a thin packet of no more than ten pages. "Look how thin it is," Dayton said. "With this, I raised $100,000. I was actually driving to meet a potential investor and I stopped at Staples, and I bought this 'Confidential!' stamp and stamped it on there." Dayton turned to the section on marketing, and read from it: 'We will compete by offering the following key points: (1) Less expensive than existing services. (2) Wider coverage than existing services. (3) Faster access than existing services. (4) Better customer service.' And that's it! That was the formula." Dayton went on, "Our early ads just said, 'We get you on the Internet.' "

EarthLink's approach was to make the Internet convenient. Dayton identified the pieces that would make his offering convenient. It had to be low-priced, but it also had to be easy to get and easy to use—i.e., wide coverage and good customer service.

Once the Internet took off in 1995, EarthLink grew 15 percent to 20 percent *a week*. EarthLink stuck to Dayton's initial formula of being easy and convenient, and emerged as one of the five biggest Internet service providers. In the long run, EarthLink failed to grab the position of *super* convenience leader. It did not offer the single easiest, most ubiquitous, habit-forming way to get on the Internet. And so EarthLink settled for an also-ran position—

behind AOL. EarthLink got off to the right start. But AOL didn't just put people on the Internet, where newly minted websites in the mid-1990s still often didn't work so well. AOL built its own content inside its service, and made it easy to navigate and use. It had the capital to offer more dial-in lines in more places than any other provider—important in the age when modems connected to the Net over phone lines. And AOL carpet-bombed the nation with free disks that could walk consumers through the process of loading AOL and getting connected. In the long slog, EarthLink couldn't match AOL's convenience. EarthLink might have been just a little too loved and not enough needed. AOL became habit, and won.

/ / /

Most of the time, a new product or service starts off inside the fidelity belly and gradually migrates out to become successful. Television, for example, exploded in the 1950s and devastated theatrical movie revenues because of convenience.

In the Depression of the 1930s, most consumers had essentially two choices if they wanted professionally produced entertainment. They could go to the movies, or they could stay home and listen to radio programs like *Amos 'n' Andy* and *Jack Armstrong, All-American Boy*. In the fidelity/convenience trade-off, movies would have been the high-fidelity winner of mass-market consumer entertainment, and radio the high-convenience winner. To see a movie, you had to go out to the theater and spend money, but you got a full visual experience. Radio was something you could enjoy at home for free, but of course it was audio only.

Television burst into the public's consciousness in 1939,

when RCA transmitted the first closed-circuit images—of President Franklin Roosevelt—at the opening ceremonies of the World's Fair in New York. Early televisions had small black-and-white screens—five or seven inches across—and extremely limited programming. The U.S. government didn't set standards for TV broadcasts until 1941, so for a while no single TV could tune in all of the approximately two dozen experimental TV stations. And TV sets cost a lot and broke down often. In the 1940s, TV was both less convenient and lower-fidelity than either radio or the movies. That position in the fidelity belly is reflected in TV sales figures. From 1940 to 1950, TVs made their way into only 3.8 million U.S. households, or about 9 percent of all homes.

But companies such as RCA and General Electric had ambitious plans for TV. It's interesting to look back at how those companies positioned television—as high-fidelity compared to radio. RCA founder David Sarnoff proclaimed, "Now we have added sight to sound." An early GE advertisement made the pitch: "Seeing things—miles away—at the very instant they happen! That's the new thrill that television now makes possible."[8] The companies were concentrating on the market for professional entertainment *in the home*—as opposed to entertainment outside the home. On that fidelity/convenience trade-off, the marketers were saying that TV was the high-fidelity choice.

But as TV developed, it took on another life as the high-convenience choice compared to movies in a theater. From 1939 to 1950, manufacturers with names such as Zenith, Philco, and Motorola entered the TV market, driving down prices. More than a hundred TV stations in sixty cities went on the air during that time, and the new government standards made sure that every TV could get reception from any station in its area. Program choices started to catch up with those available on radio. By 1950, TVs were cheap enough to be affordable and easy enough to obtain and operate, and stations offered enough good free programming to satisfy a typical consumer. TV may not have had the fidelity of movies, but it had good-enough fidelity and a lot more convenience than going out to a theater. TV started siphoning away the movies' customers.

In 1950, 3.8 million U.S. households had TVs. Within one year, the number of homes with TVs shot up to 10.3 million, or 23.5 percent. TV ownership skyrocketed through the decade. By 1960, 45.8 million homes had TVs—a whopping 87 percent of all U.S. households.[9] The effect on movies was immediate. In 1950, theaters sold a record 3 billion tickets. By 1955, ticket sales had fallen below 2.5 billion. In 1960, about half as many people—1.5 billion—went to movies as in 1950.[10]

Movies were forced to go to bigger screens, color, and special effects to compete. It's a jousting match still going on today—the reason directors like James Cameron are pushing 3-D films such as *Avatar*.

/ / /

Paul Kateman had been in the real estate business in the Boston area when his wife died of breast cancer and his business partner was killed in a plane crash. Needing to start over, Kateman decided that he had to change careers. It was the early 1990s, a time when grunge rock, Desert Storm, and a soft-serve frozen-yogurt chain called TCBY captured the headlines. The frozen-yogurt chain piqued Kateman's interest. He researched the possibility of opening a frozen-yogurt restaurant, but learned that there were difficulties with both frozen yogurt and ice cream. Frozen-yogurt machines, for instance, could make only two flavors at a time. Ice cream, meanwhile, was almost always made in large batches in a factory, stored for months, and kept at minus 20 degrees Fahrenheit as it traveled from warehouse to truck to restaurant to customers. If the temperature of ice cream creeps above minus 20, it ends up tasting like chilled Play-Doh.

As newcomers to an industry sometimes do, Kateman looked at the situation and said, "Maybe there's a different way to do this." He linked up with a Cambridge, Massachusetts, R&D firm called Product Genesis, and invented a patented process called turbulent dynamic mixing. Ice cream has always been made by slow churning, which mixes air into the freezing cream. Kateman's new process could blast air into the cream as it was flash-frozen, so ice cream could be made on the spot.

In 1992, Kateman formed a company called Turbo Dynamix. In 1995, General Mills and Turbo Dynamix entered into a joint venture to make and sell Kateman's machine to businesses. But—as sometimes happens—the big company lost interest in Turbo Dynamix and ended the venture in 1997. General Mills couldn't see where Kateman was ultimately heading. Kateman, unwilling to give up, reclaimed the technology and marshaled on.

In 2000, Kateman met Bruce Ginsberg, then CEO of New England Ice Cream. Ginsberg was a twenty-year ice-cream insider. Ginsberg believed in Turbo Dynamix and decided to join Kateman. Ginsberg, though, had one concern: "I asked Paul, 'Who in the ice-cream business is going to buy something called a turbo?'" Ginsberg told me. "Paul smiled and said, 'We should come up with a wonderful name.'" The company's few employees sat in a room and stuck words and names on a wall. One word was *moo*. Another was *bella*. "I remembered I had a dear Aunt Bella," Ginsberg says. "So we put *moo* and *bella* together." The company would be called MooBella.[11]

They scrounged up money to keep going from friends, family members, wealthy individuals, and a couple of venture capital firms. The next five years were about engineering and refining the machine—building prototypes, trying ingredients, testing the outcome. By 2006 they had a version about the size of a Coke machine. Inside were liquid dairy products in aseptic packages, which didn't have to be refrigerated. In other containers inside were flavors and add-ins such as cookies and chocolate chips. A computer running on a Linux operating system displayed menus of possible flavors on a screen at the front of the machine and allowed the user to create any combination he or she wished, such as low-fat coffee ice cream with Oreo cookies. If the machine ran out of a flavor, it stopped putting it on the menu and sent a message to MooBella asking for a refill.

For the next two years, MooBella continued to refine the machine. By late 2008, it was ready to start putting them into college cafeterias, movie theaters, hotel lobbies, and airports. MooBella has been contacted by the highway department in India, which wants to put ice-cream machines in places where you could never get ice cream: at rest stops on highways through the desert. MooBella believes it can change the ice-cream game. Using a small footprint, with relatively minimal handling, it believes it can sell dozens of flavors of freshly made ice cream in any place that has an electric outlet.

At the moment, the jury is out. But MooBella may well become the new high-convenience form of ice cream.

CHAPTER SEVEN

The Worst Place to Be

What's it like to find yourself in the depths of the fidelity belly?

Antonio Perez knows. Years after Kodak had fallen deep inside the fidelity belly, Perez was the guy who finally got Kodak to do something about it.

Perez is a charming, engaging man, with a Spanish lilt to his words, and a mischievous smile worthy of a toothpaste ad. Perez grew up in Vigo, a fishing village in Spain. His father had a fish business, and as a teenager Perez helped buy and sell the day's catch. "I only learned one thing there," Perez told me.[1] "I didn't like that business. It was cold and wet, and they were all mean people." So he got out, studying engineering and business in Spain and France and eventually landing at Silicon Valley's Hewlett-Packard, where he spent the next twenty-five years. Perez essentially built Hewlett-Packard's computer printer business. He left H-P in 1999, after the company handed the job of CEO—which Perez wanted and thought he deserved—to Carly Fiorina. In 2003, Kodak asked Perez to become its chief operating officer, with the idea that he'd learn the business and then be named CEO. He knew Kodak was getting murdered by the shift from analog film to digital photography. He took four months to study Kodak, to decide whether the job was worth attempting. He was, in effect, looking to see if Kodak had a viable path out of the fidelity belly.

Strangely enough, Kodak had invented the digital camera. In 1975, a young Kodak researcher, Steven Sasson, pieced together a clunky Rube Goldberg gadget the size of a toaster oven and persuaded a lab assistant to pose for the first digital picture. The image took twenty-three seconds to record onto a cassette tape, and another twenty-three seconds to be downloaded by a playback unit and displayed on a television set. Kodak's top management took one look at Sasson's concoction and decided it was little more than an interesting science project. But the company did patent Sasson's technology and follow-up projects—which turned out to be quite fortunate. Once digital cameras became real products, every company making them had to pay royalties to Kodak.

Kodak in the 1980s and 1990s was doing so well in film that it didn't see the dangers posed by digital photography. Kodak was wringing margins of 60 percent out of its analog film business, and in the exuberant stock market of the late 1990s, Kodak's stock hit an all-time high. But by 1999, digital camera sales were growing at a rate of nearly 40 percent a year. People who bought digital cameras stopped buying film. Kodak launched a digital camera business, but did so halfheartedly, continuing to rely on film. By the 2000s, film was clearly sinking. Starting in the summer of 1998, Kodak's stock began a long decline, from $89.75 a share to around twenty-five dollars by the mid-2000s.

By the time Perez arrived in 2003, you'd think management at Kodak would've known the company had fallen headlong into the fidelity belly. And yet, as an exasperated Perez recalls: "when I came into the company, the motto was, 'Expand the benefits of film.' There was a banner spread in my office—'Expand the benefits of film.' The first thing I did was I took that down. When I started to talk to people, my conversation with them was, 'If it can be digital, it will be digital. We can argue about the time frame, but we cannot argue about the fact.' That was the first step."

Kodak had fourteen factories around the world making film, all of them increasingly underutilized. Perez decided to close eleven of them.

"I would go to the factories, and I'd stand in front of 3,000 people," Perez told me. "Before I said my name, I would say, 'Would you please stand up if you have a digital camera in your household?' About 40 percent of the people would stand up at the beginning. And I said, 'My name is Antonio Perez. I'm your new leader, and we have a problem here. You make your living by making film here in this factory, and you're not buying it. You think anybody else is going to buy it? This cannot continue to be like this. So I'm asking for your help to do the right thing. There is no other thing to do but close the plant, so help me do it with dignity. You already know this is moving to digital, because you're already doing it.'" In recalling this, Perez paused for a beat, then said, "After I said that in two different places, it went all through the company. Next time, everybody knew I was going to say that."

As Perez made the rounds and closed factories, Kodak woke up to its position. For the first time, there was no dream of expanding the film business. Film was clearly going to become a small, niche piece of Kodak. The company's future suddenly became all about digital—and all about clawing back out of the fidelity belly.

"Action normally only happens when there is a burning platform," Perez said. "Otherwise you still live the way you used to live. It happens to all of us—human beings as well as businesses and countries." Kodak's film business had been slowly deteriorating. Perez came in and put a torch to it.

How could Kodak bounce back from its predicament? To listen to Perez, the company is trying to emphasize convenience—by making digital photography *more* convenient than it is already. Consumers can see some of that strategy in Kodak's drive to make very simple digital cameras that upload photos to computers with the push of a button. Kodak, realizing that the most convenient cameras today are the ones built into cell phones, signed a deal to co-produce camera phones with Motorola. (As of this writing, problems at Motorola have delayed those products.) But Perez seems to be thinking beyond that to something entirely new. Cameras, he said, have to be everywhere. "A camera can be in your glasses, in a ring. It can be part of anything," he told me. If Kodak can come up with new inventions that leap beyond the convenience factor of even cell-phone cameras, it stands a chance of regaining its stature in the photography arena.

That high-convenience strategy would be completely in line with Kodak's 120-year corporate culture. George Eastman built Kodak on the idea of giving average people the most convenient way to take pictures. In the 1870s, at age twenty-four, Eastman wanted to take photographs while on an overseas vacation. The only way to do it was to buy a camera as bulky as a microwave oven, and bring along chemicals, glass tanks, glass plates to expose to the light, and a tent that would act as a darkroom. Frustrated by the difficulty involved, Eastman worked for three years to make a dry photographic plate that eliminated the need for the chemicals and emulsions. It was a revolution in the convenience of photography, and it launched Eastman's company. As Kodak evolved, Eastman worked to make photography popular. In 1900, Kodak introduced the breakthrough Brownie cameras, which sold for one dollar—for the first time putting photography within the financial reach of the mass market. Kodak's advertising slogan for decades was "You press the button, we do the rest." Kodak exploded as a global brand because it offered high convenience. Yes, Kodak has long made high-end cameras and professional-quality film, but the core of the company has always been about making photography more convenient. (Remember: Like Apple, it's possible for a company to have a portfolio of both high-convenience and high-fidelity products.)

That attitude and direction seems to be what Perez is trying to recapture.

/ / /

The fidelity belly, shown on the next page, is the no-man's-land of consumer products. Movie theaters, music CDs, Blu-ray video disks, electronic book readers, electric cars, and film cameras have all found themselves in that no-man's-land.

Certainly not every company can be the absolute leader on convenience or fidelity. On that fidelity/convenience chart, most of an industry's players would be plotted all over. Some would be a little less convenient than the convenience leader, but still convenient enough to gain a sizable market. There are different ways of doing well in terms of the fidelity/convenience trade-off. For instance, few bands can put on a U2-style super-fidelity stadium rock concert with requisite lasers and explosions and set changes. But a lesser band might have success playing in smaller venues, and charging lower prices, which would make that band relatively more convenient for fans, but still a relatively high-fidelity music

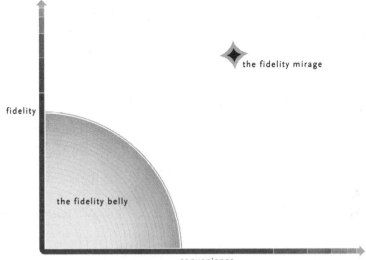

experience compared with sitting at home and listening to a ste-reo. Samsung cell phones, Sharp TVs, Sonic burger joints, and Marriott hotels are all examples of businesses that may not be either the most convenient or the highest-fidelity—but are good enough in terms of convenience or fidelity to do well.

But there is a threshold in the fidelity/convenience trade-off; cross it, and irrelevance awaits, as consumers stop feeling like they either love or need a particular a product or service. People use the product or service less frequently and look for alterna-tives. Deeper into the fidelity belly, consumers start to actively dislike a product or service, thinking it's a hassle or that it's dis-appointing compared with the available alternatives. This is how people felt about VHS tapes after experiencing DVDs.

/ / /

There is a certain kind of product or service that begins life inside the fidelity belly, and never gets out. These are flat-out losers—products or services that are ill conceived from the get-go or just plain badly made, like the Yugo or Webvan. IBM's PCjr from the 1980s was an underpowered PC that still cost a lot—so was neither convenient nor high in fidelity. Such disasters start in the belly, get some attention from early adopters and adventurous consumers, then stall, fall backward, and die. I'll look more closely at such disasters a little later on.

First, though, let's look at the products and services that begin life inside the belly and manage to get out. These are otherwise known as innovations and inventions.

The more radical inventions—the ones way ahead of current technology and consumer taste—usually start deep inside the fidelity belly, such as Steve Sasson's first digital camera. They are so expensive and impractical at that stage that no one would buy them. Cool new devices that are only a bit ahead of mass consumer behavior—like Amazon's Kindle—usually begin inside the fidelity belly, but are good enough to appeal to early adopters. Such innovations still have to find a way out of the belly to reach a mass market.

If most innovations start inside the belly, what's the difference between those that migrate out and become popular, and those—like Webvan—that never leave and ultimately die? Can you tell a Webvan from an eBay in its early stages? Or any other future success from a future failure?

Certainly a lot of smart media and tech executives suffered a lapse in judgment when the Internet TV company Joost was born.

When I visited the company at its New York office in late 2007, Joost didn't even have a sign on the door. Inside, the setting was urban hip, with exposed two-by-fours, open ductwork, and walls covered with silver stuff that looked like the lattice on a chaise lounge. I wound up talking to CEO Mike Volpi in a squished conference room furnished with cheap plastic IKEA chairs.

Joost had about twenty people in Manhattan, plus twenty in London and about sixty others spread around the world. In 2005, when the public first heard about Joost—at the time, under its code name, The Venice Project—the startup was expected to use the Internet to reinvent television. It was founded by the two guys who created Skype, Niklas Zennstrom and Janus Friis. Investors, including CBS, put up $45 million, and the company hired Mike Volpi from his high-profile position at Cisco Systems. Joost had money, clout, a reputation, and enough mystery to electrify the media. It was trying to deliver free, ad-supported, professionally produced video over the Internet in a way that protected copyrights, paid people for their work, and served up something akin to traditional TV advertising. In other words: true network television on the Web. When Joost started, no entity could do that.

The media and tech world expected Joost to be REALLY BIG—another YouTube or iTunes. But by spring of 2008, fewer than 3 million people had downloaded the software that made Joost run on a computer—which gave Joost an overall total possible audience equal to the debut episode of *Growing Up Gotti*. Joost at the time had some CBS content, while Comedy Central offered standup, the NBA served week-old games, and the most popular channels included The Sexy Clips Channel and Motors & Babes. Not exactly a TV revolution.

So what happened? Joost started out as breakthrough technology. Unfortunately, like a lot of new inventions, it started out well inside the fidelity belly. Watching shows on Joost did not provide an experience that came close to the fidelity of a nice TV set. Joost had too little popular programming, and the software was too hard for most people to install and use. As a result, Joost offered little convenience for a typical mass-market consumer.

Joost generated so much excitement from the tech cognoscenti, however, that its founders seemed to believe that consumers were going to flock to it. Joost didn't realize that it was not strong enough on fidelity or convenience for most people. And then Joost took too long to figure out how it was going to climb out of the belly.

The company needed to focus on convenience—letting people watch favorite TV shows anywhere, anytime they wanted, in a simple, easy-to-use way. This was something traditional television could not do. Television could not deliver a free, ad-supported episode of *Project Runway* to a bored traveler stuck in an airport at 3:27 in the afternoon. But Joost took too long to make its offering simple or build a sizable line-up of popular shows.

Instead, Hulu showed up and stole Joost's thunder. Formed in 2007, Hulu was backed by TV networks Fox and NBC, and run by former Amazon.com executive Jason Kilar. He made one key decision: Hulu was first and foremost about convenience. That meant no software downloads—Hulu had to run inside an Internet browser, as simply as YouTube. Hulu's website from the outset was clean and simple, and Fox and NBC populated Hulu with popular TV shows like *The Office* and *30 Rock*. As a result, momentum in Internet TV shifted to Hulu. By the time Hulu ran a Super Bowl ad in February 2009, it was on its way out of the fidelity belly. Joost was far behind.

It is too glib to say that everyone should've seen that coming.

But the Joost story illustrates what investors and managers need to look for when trying to figure out whether an innovative company or product can climb out of the belly. Management needs to ask the question, *Is our product on a clear path toward either convenience or fidelity?* If not, that suggests trouble. The surest and shortest way out of the belly is a straight line along one axis or the other.

/ / /

In the early 1990s, I dropped in to see a company called General Magic. The place had the air of a day-care center for child prodigies. Cubicles were cluttered with toys, many of them spinoffs from the recently released Disney movie *Aladdin.* A Rock 'Em Sock 'Em Robots game sat on one desk. One programmer built a bunk bed over his work space so he could stay all night. Conference rooms had names like "Yoda" and "Willy Wonka's Chocolate Factory." CEO Marc Porat dressed in black and managed with a Zen-like serenity. The other two principles—Andy Hertzfeld and Bill Atkinson—had been the chief architects who created the original Macintosh computer when they worked for Apple.

Porat, Hertzfeld, and Atkinson walked me through a tour of their project. This was before hardly anyone had heard of the Internet. Popular media were beginning to talk about a coming "information superhighway." The first browser had not yet been created, and few people had e-mail or cell phones, or bought anything online. Yet General Magic foresaw much of what the Internet was going to be—and the company was brazenly setting out to, essentially, build the whole thing.

Porat handed me a device about the size of an Etch-a-Sketch—

wirelessly connected to the cell-phone network. On the gadget's screen was a user interface that looked like a cartoonish line drawing of a street. If you wanted to read a book, you navigated down this street and went into a door marked "Library." If you wanted to play a game, you went into a game room. To do work-related things, you navigated to a desk. No network-based services or websites existed yet, so General Magic created a software agent, called Telescript, which was supposed to reside in the computers of travel agencies and news operations and so on. The Telescript inside your device was supposed to talk to the Telescript inside companies' computers to make transactions. As I wrote after my visit to General Magic:

> *Say you call up the agent on your computer (or PDA or set-top box) and tell it that you want it to buy two round-trip plane tickets to Portland, Maine, on a certain date, plus get a compact rental car and a downtown hotel room. You connect to a travel network, send the agent into it, and immediately disconnect. When the agent finds what you asked for, it dials you up, comes back to your computer, and shows you the choices it has found. You check off what you want, give the agent your credit card number, authorize it to make the purchases, then send it back into the network. Telescript is like having someone to run errands for you.* [2]

Again—none of the infrastructure existed to make any of that work. But it sure sounded like a great idea to a lot of smart executives. AT&T invested in General Magic and started to try to put Telescript on a proprietary Internet-like network it called PersonaLink. Japan's phone giant, NTT, invested too. So did Motorola and Sony, and each built handheld devices intended to run General Magic's software. Other backers of General Magic included France Telecom, Philips, Matsushita, Toshiba, and Fujitsu. For top engineers and programmers, General Magic became the hottest place to work in Silicon Valley.

And yet the whole concept was so far ahead of its time, General Magic began life deep inside the fidelity belly—like Steve Sasson's first digital camera. Even if it all worked back in 1993, the hurdles for almost any potential user were huge—from the cost of buying the necessary devices to learning how to use this stuff without ever having touched anything like it before, to the total lack of comfort with the whole concoction. Convenience? Out of the question. It would be years and many iterations of technology before the mass market would find this stuff convenient. Fidelity? Not a chance. It would be years before the computing power, networks, software, and online services got to a point of offering anything approaching a great experience. Was there at least a pathway toward convenience or fidelity? Nope. General Magic didn't have one. Porat and crew were making technology—which was inarguably cool and prescient—for technology's sake. Seen through the lens of the fidelity/convenience trade-off, General Magic seemed hopeless. A brilliant idea, but with no hope of achieving fidelity or convenience, there was no way out of the fidelity belly. And yet a boatload of corporate giants invested millions of dollars in it.

General Magic didn't amount to much as a business. (It later morphed into a voice-recognition company, although the original version of General Magic and its concept were kaput by 1996.) But General Magic's mere existence put its ideas into the ether, which helped ratchet the tech industry toward the Internet we know today. If General Magic's investors had thought about fidelity and convenience, I wonder if they would have been as starry-eyed, and would have written those checks.

It's fascinating, though, how a core part of General Magic's business idea evolved over the following fifteen years. By the end of the 2000s, the concept of agents—of a system that would do things on your behalf—finally stood a chance of breaking out of the fidelity belly. In 2008, I sat at a conference table across from Patrick Grady, CEO of Rearden Commerce, in the company's Silicon Valley headquarters. He had carefully tracked General Magic all those years ago, and was taken with its concept of an agent acting as a kind of personal assistant. Grady watched Hewlett-Packard and then Microsoft both launch efforts in the late 1990s and early 2000s to succeed where General Magic failed. A few years later, both of those behemoths pretty much shelved their projects, unable to make them work. Grady, though, formed Rearden and kept hammering at the problem.

During that time, the entire Internet and computing ecosystem had evolved. The Internet had grown up, and consumers were becoming used to smart sites—often dubbed "Web 2.0"—that could work with other sites across the Web. Online commerce had become common. Handheld devices, like the iPhone and BlackBerry, had grown sophisticated. All the pieces so absent in General Magic's day were in place.

That allowed Grady to see a path out, and the path was all about convenience. As he explained to me that day, he sees Rearden playing out a fidelity/convenience trade-off in a category that might be labeled "personal assistance." In such a category or market, the high-fidelity solution is a top-notch human personal assistant. But most people can't afford a personal assistant. So they do most everything themselves, because there really is no high-convenience solution—no version of a personal assistant that is cheap, ubiquitous, and easy to use.

The technology ecosystem is finally making the idea of a personal, Web-based agent possible for ordinary people. Rearden's technology can, for instance, achieve the travel scenario that General Magic described in the early 1990s. In the mid-2000s, Rearden started selling software to corporate travel departments to prove the point. Once investors saw that the technology worked, Rearden got $100 million in funding from American Express, J.P. Morgan Chase, and venture capitalists. That's a huge vote of confidence. Chase plans to offer Rearden's travel "agent" to its millions of credit-card customers. Not far down the road, Rearden-powered agents should be able to do a lot more than pull together travel arrangements. One simple example: Your agent might watch all your Web-based social networks for birthdays of friends and family members, notify you when one is coming, check their favorite shopping sites for "wish list" items, and offer you a few possible gifts to send them, all with a simple click.

As happened with Kodak's invention of the digital camera, Joost's Internet TV service, and General Magic, good ideas can sit inside the fidelity belly for a long time, and never ultimately pan out for the originator. Success often comes about when someone finally sees a path out of the belly to the market beyond.

/ / /

Because the tech effect constantly moves the borders outward on both convenience and fidelity, a product or service doesn't have to decline or become worse to fall into the belly—it only has to stand still or fail to keep pace with improving technology.

I know how this looks from the inside. I worked at a newspaper for twenty-two years.

Newspapers, obviously, are in the business of news. For much of the past fifty years, newspapers were the convenience leaders of news, compared with all the other ways people could get news: magazines, TV, documentaries, books—or the ultimate high-fidelity news source, being there yourself. Newspapers, in their heyday, had the hallmarks of high convenience. They were cheap, ubiquitous, familiar, and easy to use. A lot of people might not have loved their newspapers, but most citizens felt they needed them. In fact, newspapers became a habit—an ultimate sign of high convenience.

Newspapers also operate in a market that's a subset of broadly defined news. That market is *deadline* news. It's the business of informing people about events like disasters, baseball games, and elections soon after they happen. Competitors in timely news, until the mid-1990s, included radio, TV, word of mouth—and not much else. There were few other sources of deadline news. When viewing the market this way, newspapers were typically a high-fidelity product, usually offering deeper, more-nuanced coverage compared with the more immediate coverage of, say, the local TV station.

In either bucket, newspapers occupied a strong position—best in convenience in "news" and best in fidelity in "deadline news." Because of that, most newspapers enjoyed robust revenue and profit margins for much of their existence. Gannett, the biggest newspaper company in the United States—and my employer for those twenty-two years—saw its stock steadily increase through most of its history. Its biggest run-up started in 1985, just after I joined the company. The good performance ended abruptly in about 2005, and the stock has since gone off a cliff.

Why? Well, it's no secret that the Internet changed the game for newspapers. The fidelity/convenience swap helps to explain why the Internet's arrival was so devastating—and how newspapers might yet respond.

In the "news" bucket, Internet-based news usurped newspapers' mantle of convenience. Web news didn't accomplish that the minute it arrived on the scene in the mid-1990s. It took time until the general population had computers, broadband, always-on connections, and a general comfort level with the Web. By 2005, Internet news had become more convenient than newspapers for much of the population. It was right there on the computers people were already working on or using for e-mail, and Web news had become easy to use, well-packaged—and *free*. This was the tech effect at work. Newspapers didn't necessarily get worse, but they did either stand still as a news medium, or get only slightly better. Newspapers reluctantly put up websites, and in many cases the sites were not very good. Technology pushed out the borders of what was possible in news delivery, and sites like Yahoo News and blogs leaped past newspapers in convenience. Newspapers stood relatively still as the borders of the fidelity belly pushed past them, leaving newspapers neither convenient enough to be needed, nor high-fidelity enough to be loved. For many people, particularly a younger generation, the habit was gone.

How did newspapers fare in the "deadline news" bucket? As the Internet age unfolded, newspapers felt they held a fidelity trump card. The thinking among editors went: "Okay, the Internet might offer more convenient news, but it's mostly unsophisticated news bites. Anyway, people don't want to read in-depth stories on computer screens. So there's still a place for the fidelity of professional, thoughtful, objective, fact-checked newspaper stories in print."

That was true until a few things happened. As the news audience started shifting from newspapers to the Web, so did advertising—especially classified ads for jobs, used cars, and other items. At the same time, news on the Web got better and deeper. Internet news sites grew up. They hired more professional journalists. Consumers, meanwhile, became more comfortable with reading stories on screens. All these things were coming together at once. Finally, newspapers nailed shut their own coffin. As revenue started moving from newspapers to the Web, newspapers cut staff, closed bureaus, trimmed the size of their editions, and day by day whittled down the fidelity of the print product. (In 2008 the *Washington Post* and *New York Times* each cut about 100 news staffers; the *Arizona Republic* cut twenty-seven; the *Olympian* in Olympia, Washington, cut four of its forty-five newsroom employees; and similar layoffs were happening in every corner of the industry. If anything, cuts sped up in 2009.)

By the early 2000s, daily newspapers no longer had sole possession of the high-fidelity hilltop in the "deadline news" bucket. Newspapers were made worse while Web news got better. Newspapers reached 57 percent of U.S. households in 1999; by 2006 it was 50 percent and falling quickly.[3]

Is there a way to turn around and get back out of the fidelity belly? Possibly. The shortest route out is to strive for either high convenience, or high fidelity. That might mean redefining the product or service in a way that gives it a shot at regaining a high-fidelity position, or a high-convenience position.

Here's one possible strategy: The newspaper industry has always thought of itself as producing a mass-market product, appealing to all demographics. But the attitude toward newspapers is radically different among different age groups. In 2006, only 35 percent of Americans age eighteen to twenty-four read newspapers. But 54 percent of people forty-five to fifty-four read newspapers, going up to 67 percent of those over sixty-five.[4]

Older-generation readers tend to subscribe to newspapers for fidelity reasons—to them, the newspaper is a good experience. And those are the readers newspapers stand to lose by putting out a disappointing product. It might be worthwhile to redefine print newspapers as a high-fidelity product aimed specifically at an audience forty-five and older. Forget trying to do stories to lure young readers—instead print more stories about anti-aging tactics, high-end local restaurants, business, politics, and other topics important to baby boomers and their elders. No newspaper, to my knowledge, has tried such a strategy. Most are still trying to figure out how to sell a print product to younger people who are abandoning it—and who are unlikely to ever see a print newspaper as either highly convenient or high fidelity.

There is another option: Kill the print product altogether, and put the newspaper's professional journalists on a course to become the high-fidelity news source on the Web—in other words, the high-fidelity option in the "deadline news" bucket. This is a strategy announced in late 2008 by the *Christian Science Monitor*.

I had a conversation about this strategy with Marc Andreessen, who cofounded Netscape Communications in the 1990s and went on to start or fund dozens of Web media companies including Twitter, Ning, and Qik. Andreessen also writes a blog that is popular with the tech crowd. In early 2008 he famously initiated what he called his *"New York Times* deathwatch." So I asked him what he'd do if he owned the *Times*.

"Shut off the print edition right now," he told me. "You've got to play offense. The financial markets have discounted forward to the terminal conclusion for newspapers, which is basically bankruptcy. And so at this point, if you're one of these major newspapers and you shut off the printing press, your stock price would probably go up, despite the fact that you would lose 90 percent of your revenue. Then you play offense and, guess what, you're an Internet company." Andreessen acknowledges that "to be the generation of owners or managers of newspapers who have to shut off the printing presses after like five hundred years—I'm sure that's going to be emotional." But it may be one of the few choices newspaper companies can make to get out of the fidelity belly.

/ / /

In the mid-1990s, Apple Computer was a wreck. Cofounder and spiritual leader Steve Jobs had been driven out in 1985. The company lost its way under different CEOs trying to sell more-generic computers to corporations and less capable computers to consumers. Under one CEO, John Sculley, Apple created the Newton handheld computer. A global phenomenon when introduced, it turned into a gigantic flop because it went against the very core of the Steve Jobs religion of making "insanely great" products. The Newton was a buggy nightmare with a terrible user interface and limited capabilities.

In early 1996, not long after Apple reported a $68-million

loss for the fourth quarter of 1995, I met up with the company's CEO at the time, Gil Amelio. He had spent most of the day at a technology conference answering questions about how he was changing Apple. Throughout the day, this sober corporate character wore a suit and tie, which by itself marked a huge culture clash with the rest of the company. Listening to him over lunch, I found Amelio's ideas for Apple entirely pragmatic—but not in the least bit sexy. Nothing had the ring or reverberation of Steve Jobs thumbing his nose at IBM and saying Apple was building "a computer for the rest of us."

Back in 1984, Apple had claimed the personal computer industry's high-fidelity position when it introduced the Macintosh. Windows computers were the workaday, ho-hum machines. Macs were an *experience*. Like all great fidelity products, it gave its owners a sense of identity. Mac owners were artists and freethinkers and anything but corporate drones. In 1996, Amelio's mere presence at the helm showed that Apple had given up on its fidelity and instead lost its way and wound up in the fidelity belly. Its products weren't cheap and ubiquitous enough to be high convenience, and they had stopped being cool enough to be high fidelity.

Apple is proof that a company can fall into the belly yet find its way back out. In late 1996, Amelio's Apple bought Steve Jobs's company NeXT, and Jobs came back to Apple. Jobs guided the company back toward high fidelity. Every product had to be a wonderful experience. Apple produced sleeker and better Macs and PowerBook laptops and once again cultivated that sense of identity—notably with its "Think Different" ad campaign. Apple became the fidelity leader of personal computers—and then it took that mind-set to other arenas, like the competitive and crowded arena of cell phones. Apple's iPhone leaped instantly to the high-fidelity position among all existing cell phones.

Jobs is a brilliant product designer and marketer. But the best thing he did for Apple was to refocus the company on fidelity.

CHAPTER EIGHT

The Worst Thing to Try

Starbucks hit a wall in 2007. Fewer people were coming into its stores. Profits sank. The stock dropped by nearly half through the year. In early 2008, Howard Schultz, who'd built the coffee chain into a global phenomenon, took back the CEO job he'd relinquished eight years before. And almost everything he said about what went wrong points to one simple explanation: Starbucks chased the fidelity mirage.

Starbucks, during its heyday, was about fidelity. Schultz became enamored with the coffee business while selling Swedish-designed kitchen equipment for Perstorp. That led him to visit Starbucks when it was a tiny specialty coffee-bean roaster in Seattle. He signed on as an employee, went to Milan on a business trip, and discovered Italian espresso bars with their rich brews, overwhelming aroma, elegant traditions, and neighborhood camaraderie. It all gelled into an epiphany for Schultz: "If [Starbucks] could re-create in America the authentic Italian coffee bar culture, it might resonate with other Americans the way it did with me," Schultz wrote in his autobiography, *Pour Your Heart Into It*. "Starbucks could be a great *experience,* and not just a great retail store."[1]

Schultz bought Starbucks from its founders in 1987. If you look back on what he was thinking in those early days, you can see that it was all about creating a high-fidelity experience that was greater than just the coffee. He wanted Starbucks stores to have "a taste of romance" and be "an oasis—a small escape during a day when so many other things are beating you down." He saw Starbucks stores as a "third place" in people's lives—a feelgood social gathering spot, the role played by pubs in England and teahouses in Japan. It's what Cheers was on the TV show of the same name—where everybody knows your name, or at least treats you as if they do.[2] Schultz's insight brought social meaning to Starbucks—it became an accelerator that gave the Starbucks experience that much more fidelity.

And the products Starbucks served? While Schultz always believed that the coffee had to be special, that was probably the least of Starbucks' attraction. Starbucks' other beverages and the rituals they spawned—the ordering of half-caf skinny double lattes—were at first intriguing and luxurious. Eventually they became a cultural touchstone. Once Starbucks arrived on the scene, it suddenly seemed boring to walk into a deli or a Dunkin' Donuts and just order coffee with cream and sugar.

When it was fresh and new in the world's consciousness, Starbucks had a special aura. The green label on a cardboard cup made the coffee it held seem better. Saying you were going to make a run to Starbucks got your coworkers' attention in a way that saying "I'm going to get coffee" never did. Holding that Starbucks coffee cup, being seen in a Starbucks, and being enough of a regular that you knew your favorite complex beverage combination off the top of your head conferred a bit of identity. You were one of the cool people who treated yourself with the highestquality coffee beverages available.

For all of this, Starbucks charged premium prices. A cup of Starbucks coffee cost at least twice as much as the same size cup elsewhere. The fancier drinks, like espressos and lattes and macchiatos, cost three or four or five dollars a cup. As coffee goes, there was essentially nothing convenient about Starbucks. You had to travel to find one, wait in line, and pay exorbitant prices for a product you could make at home or in the office for relatively nothing. But that didn't matter. Schultz had put together everything needed to create a high-fidelity experience. Few businesses executed high fidelity in their product so well. And that is why the Starbucks brand exploded onto the scene in the late 1990s.

Schultz then did what any ambitious entrepreneur would be driven to do: he took full advantage of the love shown Starbucks and launched aggressive expansion plans. Starbucks shareholders demanded it. But that behavior can lead to the very thing that can kill a high-fidelity brand: familiarity.

Which is exactly what happened to Starbucks. As the economist Tyler Cowen told me, "Once Starbucks became ordinary, it was committing suicide."[3]

Starbucks saturated the world with its franchises. In urban areas, Starbucks stores seemed to land on every corner, in every mall, next to every highway interchange. The 2004 animated movie *Shrek 2* made a visual joke that involves a Starbucks-like store getting destroyed, while the customers flee into an identical store directly across the street. The satirical newspaper *The Onion* published a headline: NEW STARBUCKS OPENS IN RESTROOM OF EXISTING STARBUCKS. Schultz retired as CEO in 2000 (though he remained as chairman), and the next two CEOs pushed expansion plans even harder, while extending the Starbucks brand to include ice cream, packaged beverages, and a record label. In 1998 the world was populated with 1,886 Starbucks stores. Ten

years later there were 16,226. Schultz blessed it all, convinced
that Starbucks could be everywhere and still be special.

"I would never allow Starbucks to sacrifice or downgrade
its elegance and style for the sake of growth," Schultz wrote in
1997. "As we grow bigger, we can afford to invest in the kind of
creative, innovative design that pushes the envelope. That's how
we'll maintain the edge of surprise and delight that has always
been a hallmark of the Starbucks experience."[4]

Seen through the fidelity/convenience trade-off, Schultz and
his successors started Starbucks with high fidelity; but their expansion plans went in the opposite direction, toward high convenience. Essentially, they believed Starbucks could be both at
the same time. They wanted Starbucks to be available at every
moment, everywhere. At the same time, they wanted Starbucks
to be a unique, feel-good experience that conferred upon its
customers a sense of identity. Starbucks wanted to be loved *and*
needed. And that is nearly impossible.

Starbucks saw the mirage and went for it. But it's a journey
that ends badly. Convenience acts like antimatter to fidelity. The
more convenient something becomes—the easier it is to get—
the more its aura dissipates. The more convenient something becomes, the less that item identifies its owner as someone unique
and special. For Starbucks, excessive convenience dragged down
the brand and made it commonplace.

On the flip side, Starbucks could not achieve genuine convenience while attempting to hold on to its sense of fidelity. The
prices of Starbucks' products were too high, and Starbucks had
another convenience problem: lines. Making fancy customized
drinks like frappuccinos tied up the baristas, causing back-
ups. Customers realized that if they were looking for a quick,

good-enough cup of coffee, it was easier to go to McDonald's or 7-Eleven, and save a few bucks.

One clear signal to me that Starbucks had gone off course was when it opened a compact stand in 2007 inside my neighborhood supermarket, not more than twenty yards from a full-blown Starbucks. It went against everything that Schultz originally envisioned. A stand plunked in a grocery store can't offer customers that special place and social context. It was a glorified vending machine. Serving coffee to a customer who would stick it in a cupholder on a shopping cart was hardly a luxurious experience.

Starbucks' customers reacted predictably. Despite more Starbucks stores than ever before, people started veering away. In 2007, same-store traffic slipped for the first time in Starbucks' history. People looking for convenience saw less reason to pay Starbucks' prices. People looking for aura and identity turned back to smaller chains or independent local coffee shops. In mid-2008, Dale Roberts, owner of the independent Java Shack in Arlington, Virginia, reported that his sales were growing by double digits while Starbucks stumbled. "I think there is a surge of people wanting to go back and feel at home with coffee," he told the *Washington Post*.[5]

Most people know this feeling instinctively. When anything—a brand, a rock band, a style of clothing—becomes popular with a huge mass market, the cool people increasingly find it uncool, and look for something new.

In February 2007, Schultz could see what was happening to his company. He wrote a memo to then-CEO Jim Donald, deploring "the watering down of the Starbucks experience" and "the commoditization of our brand." In January 2008, Schultz booted Donald out and took back the CEO position. He immediately began reaching backward, toward Starbucks' high-fidelity core. He told CNBC's Maria Bartiromo that Starbucks would "go back to our roots and reaffirm our leadership position as the world's highest-quality purveyor of specialty coffee." Schultz added, "It reminds me of the old days when our company was very creative, very entrepreneurial, and we were fighting for survival and respect."[6]

By the middle of the year, he admitted that Starbucks' aura had suffered. "We're not this young, beloved, entrepreneurial enterprise anymore," Schultz said. "We have to do business in a different way."[7]

Schultz got a lot of media attention for two dramatic moves. First, he shut down 7,000 Starbucks stores for three hours so that 135,000 baristas could learn how to correctly make a Starbucks espresso. (Whether they really needed to get that training or not, the move sent a message to the public that Starbucks was serious about quality.) Second, Schultz announced that 600 Starbucks outlets in the United States would close.[8] Though that's only about 5 percent of the total—and Starbucks had plans to open 350 new stores in different locations—the move marked the first time Starbucks backed away from its drive for convenience.

Will Schultz be able to help Starbucks regain its luster? It could be tough. As economist Cowen pointed out, for a brand like Starbucks, familiarity and ubiquity are deadly. The aura and identity Starbucks once had is gone for most Americans. It doesn't mean people will stop going to Starbucks. But it does mean people will stop *seeking out* Starbucks. Coffee purveyors that are more convenient (like McDonald's or 7-Eleven) or are perceived as higher fidelity (independent coffee shops or smaller chains) will have an easier time competing against Starbucks than they used to.

/ / /

Apple's iPhone may be the undoing of the Apple brand—if Steve Jobs follows the same path as Starbucks' Howard Schultz.

In the 2000s, Jobs made Apple into *the* super-fidelity tech company. Apple kept prices high, made products that ignored the convenience of working well with open standards and other companies' products, and made hardware and software that was beautifully designed and crafted and undeniably better than competing products. Those elements alone would make Apple an admirable company. But Apple always had a secret sauce that was key to its success: its aura and identity. Apple for most of its existence was the underdog, fighting Goliaths like Microsoft and IBM. With Steve Jobs back at the helm, Apple was cool, creative, rebellious, sexy. Apple created a powerful brand. Even hard-nosed reviewers seemed to think its products were cooler just because they were from Apple. More important, Apple conferred identity. If you owned something from Apple, you were one of the cognoscenti who knew better. You were smarter, more hip. That is pretty powerful stuff. Steve Jobs has proven to be a master at keeping that image going.

In 2001, Apple introduced the iPod and iTunes. At first these were typical Apple high-fidelity products—expensive, better than anything else on the market, totally cool. But then something odd happened for Apple—something Apple had never before experienced: its product was desired by the masses. Apple, seizing the opportunity, went with it, cutting prices and ramping up production. The company created the iPod Nano to serve even a broader, lower end of the market. Then it created the Shuffle to expand the market even more. Apple at one point had more than 90 percent of the digital-music-player market. Apple drove to make the iPod convenient—until the iPod achieved that pinnacle of super-convenience: it became a habit. The iPod was the music player to buy when you didn't want to think about what music player to buy. And although the iPods worked wonderfully, by 2008 they were no longer necessarily better than every other music player. Microsoft poured development money into its Zune player and came up with innovative features that were absent from iPods. Companies such as SanDisk did the same. But nothing seemed to be able to dent the iPod's market share. Apple's software made music bought on iTunes hard to play on any other device, so buying a new iPod when your old one broke was easier than the alternative. By the late 2000s, tens of millions of people owned iPods. They became ubiquitous.

And iPods became blasé. An iPod stopped conferring identity some time ago. It didn't make you cool. It only made you fit in. It no longer had a special aura. For people who wanted portable music, the iPod became more needed than loved.

This could have been a huge problem for Apple. The company still made and sold millions of laptop and desktop computers, but it was becoming best known for the iPod and iTunes. The more mass-market the music products became, the less Apple could be the company of "Think Different." Its aura was at risk. If that seems crazy to say, imagine Apple today if it never invented the iPhone. It would be making computers and iPods— neither getting people all that excited anymore. The public would increasingly see Apple as tired and less cool. Stretched between the super-convenience of the iPod and a desire to keep the Mac at high fidelity, Apple as a brand would have been dangerously chasing the mirage.

By 2004, according to a *Wired* magazine report, Jobs realized the iPod left Apple vulnerable. Smart phones like the Palm Treo and Research In Motion's BlackBerry were capturing consumers' imagination.[9] Such high-end cell phones soon would have enough storage to hold and play digital music in addition to making calls and handling e-mail. They'd make stand-alone iPods seem even less exciting and more of a commodity. To counter this, Jobs at first cut a deal to make a music cell phone with Motorola called ROCKR, but the ROCKR was mediocre, and never sold well. So Jobs gave up on Motorola, and instructed his engineers to create a touch-screen handheld computer that could be a music player, cell phone, and all-around digital device, all in one.

In January 2007, on stage at Apple's Macworld conference in San Francisco, Jobs unveiled the iPhone—and recaptured Apple's position as a company of super-fidelity. The iPhone—with its touch screen, built-in Wi-Fi, and breakthrough user interface—was instantly the highest-fidelity cell phone on the market. It cost, at first, a whopping $599. But that didn't matter to Apple enthusiasts. The iPhone brought back the company's aura and identity. An iPhone could make its owner feel cooler and smarter than everyone else. Thousands of people lined up outside Apple Stores for days before the iPhone first went on sale in June 2007. Apple sold 5 million iPhones before 2007 ended, and more than 10 million in 2008. The iPhone quickly become Apple's centerpiece product. The iPhone gave Apple its image back.

But that's only the beginning of the story. As I write this, Apple stands at one of those proverbial crossroads—much like Starbucks in the early 1990s. The company has invented a game-changing mobile device and, in the process, unleashed a great deal of pent-up demand. For the iPhone's first year on the market, Apple sold them in the United States only through Apple stores or AT&T stores. In September 2008, iPhones went on sale in Best Buy's 970 U.S. stores, making iPhones far more easily accessible to the mass market. That month, I interviewed Web pioneer Marc Andreessen in front of a gathering of Silicon Valley's Churchill Club. He held up his iPhone, declared that the product had changed the course of mobile communications, and adamantly predicted that Apple would sell 100 million iPhones.[10] That's equal to the number of RAZR cell phones that Motorola had sold, which had made RAZR the most popular mobile device in history.

Apple could probably do it, if it dropped iPhone prices further, ramped up manufacturing and marketing, and flooded iPhones into retail channels, just as Motorola had with RAZR. But that strategy killed RAZR's fidelity, and brutally damaged the brand.

Apple can't achieve both fidelity and convenience with the iPhone. Trying to drive a high-fidelity product toward high convenience kills its exclusiveness, its coolness, the aura and the identity that captivate consumers. Apple will have to decide whether it wants to maintain the iPhone as a high-end, exclusive luxury product—à la the Mac computers—or drive it through to the mass market and make it as common and necessary as the iPod.

The choice here could determine what kind of company Apple becomes. If it sells 100 million iPhones, Apple will evolve into a tech giant, and consumers will view the company differently. It's easy to love an underdog; it's a little harder to love a dynasty. Apple could hold onto its cachet—but only if it pulls off another iPhone. Just as the iPhone gave Apple back its mojo when the iPod became common, some new invention will have to do the same if the iPhone becomes commonplace. Apple can succeed making high-convenience products, but its brand demands to have high-fidelity products in its portfolio.

Apple has another choice: It could put the brakes on iPhone distribution, pump money into iPhone R&D so Apple always offers the highest-fidelity mobile gadget, keep prices high, and maintain the aura and identity that make people so crazy about Apple. The company wouldn't grow as big, but it would maintain its outsized influence on the industry and society. This is closer to Apple's core—to what it knows how to be.

/ / /

In choked Beijing traffic, I sat in a Hyundai Sonata with seats covered in spotless white cloth. Beijing National Stadium, nick-named "the bird's nest," loomed out the right-side window, the centerpiece of the city's 2008 Summer Olympics. Two Ameri-can PR guys fidgeted in the Hyundai's passenger seats. They got more nervous as each minute passed. We were on our way to meet with Bill Amelio, U.S.-born CEO of Lenovo, China's big-gest technology company. And we were running late. The Chi-nese driver, trying to nudge through a toll booth, played chicken with Volkswagens, Citroëns, buses, cement trucks, and slender, Chinese-made microvans. We could've walked faster.

Amelio was, by reputation, impatient and tough. He had whipped Lenovo into shape in his first two years at the helm. Making him wait was probably a bad thing.

We squeezed past the toll booth, a salute to China's abun-dance of labor. At least twenty workers stood around in orange vests, doing nothing but looking at the cars. We gained a bit of speed as we went past another reminder of the nation's unfathomable mass of humanity: construction cranes assembling nearly identical forty-story-plus apartment buildings as far as the eye could see—which was not all that far, thanks to Beijing's persistent white smog.

Turning off the highway, we mixed with bicycles, cars, and scooters, passing a building named, in English, WOOL SPINNING CITY and a watermelon stand. We were ten minutes late, going on fifteen. The Hyundai turned into an area that could've been a clone of a Silicon Valley corporate park, if most employees rode to work on their grandfathers' bikes. One of the PR guys text-messaged our position to headquarters. Finally the car pulled up to Lenovo's front door. We piled out like commandos. Go, go, go! Through Lenovo's glass-and-steel lobby, past a fountain, across a campus, up the elevators, into an open space of low cubicles, around a corner, into a tidy conference room set aside for the interview—and Amelio was not there.

"He's in traffic," a petite young woman in a dress apologized. "There was an accident."

Everyone let out a long breath.

In the mid-2000s, as national economies go, China was all about high convenience. It offered the developed world massive manufacturing capabilities at very low cost. Importantly, China in the 1990s and 2000s made it easy—even routine—for Western companies to manufacture in Chinese plants. That fueled China's economic miracle, lifting it up from its isolated, Communist past. Yet, as often happens when incomes and education rise, China wanted more respect. China was mainly respected for its massive size, like the deference you'd pay to Mike Tyson in a barroom. China desperately wanted respect for its brains and quality and class. In short, China wanted more fidelity. A lot of fidelity.

China at first counted on an American—Amelio—to help. The nation had a five-year government program, ratified in March 2006, to create a knowledge-led, innovation-oriented economy. In the short term, China needed a global breakout brand to serve notice that the country had arrived at the highest levels of competition. Sony did it for post–World War II Japan. Samsung led the way for South Korea in the 1990s. Nokia put Finland on the map. "That Lenovo becomes an international brand is of vital importance to China," Chen Lin, senior analyst at Beijing's CCID Consulting, told me. "It signifies that China is climbing to the upstream of the industry chain."

At Lenovo's Beijing headquarters, Amelio finally strode into the conference room after his morning traffic debacle, apparently unruffled. He didn't flinch when asked if he felt the pressure of the burden of carrying China to a new level. "I don't feel any pressure about that," he said, eyes confidently fixed, a grin making him look slightly amused. "One of the exciting reasons I took this job is that this hasn't been done before."

China is the first nation to strive for the fidelity mirage. As a 2006 report from the consulting firm Accenture so perfectly put it: "China's goals are no different from those of other countries that aspire to move up the value chain. But it is the *first* country trying to concurrently maintain a vast manufacturing base . . . and build on its ability to provide the world with high-value goods and services."[11] China wants to migrate from super-convenience toward super-fidelity, hoping it can capture both.

There is a well-worn path for nations to follow that want to move from high convenience to high fidelity. Think of Japan. After World War II, the nation rebuilt itself on cheap manufacturing. In the 1960s, the label "Made in Japan" became common on inexpensive toys and clothes sold in the West. Starting with companies like Sony and Toyota, Japan moved through the 1970s and 1980s from a nation of low-end goods to one of innovative, high-tech, high-end products. The country's economy soared, with wages and real estate prices shooting to the top of global levels. In 1980, Japan's per capita gross national product was US$9,068. In 1990 it was up to US$23,801. By the 2000s, most of the electronics designed and sold by Japanese companies were manufactured elsewhere in Asia, where labor was cheaper.

South Korea more recently followed a similar path, led by Samsung, Hyundai, and LG. Lately it's been India's turn. In the early 2000s, India made itself into the world's super-convenient player for cheap, low-end information technology services—data entry, small programming tasks, call centers, and so on. By the end of the decade, companies such as Infosys were moving up the value chain, as the consultants say—toward creating their own products and brands instead of doing outsourced work for Western companies. India as a nation is striving to rise to a higher-end role in the global economy. No longer wanting to offer products and services that are simply needed, it wants to offer products and services that are loved.

Japan and Korea didn't attempt to hold on to a low-cost manufacturing base. They didn't strive for both fidelity and convenience at once. A nation moves up the value chain—moves toward fidelity—by pumping money into education and generally raising the level of knowledge and competitiveness as broadly as possible across the population. A more-educated public expects better jobs and higher wages. Paying higher wages erodes a nation's convenience—it might still be easy and efficient to manufacture or do low-level information work, but it would cost more. Reaching toward fidelity automatically makes a country less convenient. Of course, it takes years—decades—to drag an entire economy toward fidelity, and for a long time there would continue to be plenty of people at the bottom of the knowledge pool, willing to accept low wages while more-educated citizens at the top of the knowledge pool break through on fidelity—à la Bill Amelio's Lenovo. Eventually, though, the whole nation's fidelity and income rise, and the nation prices itself out of high-convenience manufacturing. And so the world economy finds another emerging super-convenient manufacturer.

China is so vast, with such a huge population, that its journey from convenience to fidelity is certain to take decades. To use another analogy, China is like a train one thousand miles long. As the locomotive pulls into the first stop on the way to fidelity, half the train still hasn't left the convenience station. Ultimately, if China wants to rise to fidelity, it will have to relinquish its hold on convenience. With a percentage of the population in high-paying, globally competitive jobs, and a bulge left far behind in low-wage subsistence jobs, China would find itself in a potentially volatile situation. The Chinese seem to know this. A column in *China Daily* by Liang Hongfu, titled "Move Up the Value Chain," argued, "Maintaining a lower salary structure than the competitors is hardly a sound policy in the high-end marketplace."[12] China will likely span fidelity and convenience for a long time to come, but it will probably find that it is impossible to hold on to both.

/ / /

Managers running a high-convenience operation face pressure to increase margins, so they chase fidelity. Managers running a high-fidelity operation face pressure to boost growth, so they chase convenience.

In the spring of 2005, Harvard Business School's publication *Working Knowledge* effused about mass luxury in an article titled "Selling Luxury to Everyone." It started out, "Luxury is the new essential. Consumers know it and retailers are reaping the bounty."[13]

Companies such as Burberry and Jaguar chased it. Designers like Isaac Mizrahi signed a deal to supply clothes to Target. Earlier, we saw how Coach was seduced by the mass luxury siren call. Even Tiffany got sucked in. Long one of the most exclusive luxury brands in the world, Tiffany in the late 1990s tried extending its brand downward. The company began selling silver bracelet charms for $110. In no time, Tiffany retail shops were jammed with an entirely new kind of customer: middle-class teenage girls. Tiffany's sales exploded, jumping 67 percent from 1997 to 2002. Stockholders loved it and pressured the company to keep up the strategy. But Tiffany executives began to worry about the long-term damage to the brand. Mark Aaron, Tiffany's vice president of investor relations, told the *Wall Street Journal* in 2007, "What if some of those teenagers fill up their jewelry boxes with Tiffany silver, and as they get older, they perceive Tiffany as where they got their teenage jewelry?"

As the fidelity/convenience tradeoff shows, "mass luxury" is a fallacy. Mass is about convenience, and luxury is about fidelity. They can't coexist. Luxury without exclusivity becomes common. "Mass luxury" is really just about raising the bar of daily existence, setting a new standard of quality and experience that much of the population expects. At that point it is, by definition, no longer a luxury.

People naturally look for ways to identify their socioeconomic place in the world. The very wealthy do it with luxury. When something that's luxurious and exclusive today becomes commonplace, the very wealthy redefine luxury, seeking products or services that are out of reach of the rest of the population.

Because of the tech effect, as the boundaries of fidelity and convenience constantly move outward, whatever is high fidelity today—or is the most luxurious today—becomes superseded tomorrow by something of greater fidelity. And today's high-fidelity product or service drops down a few notches and becomes more everyday.

In 1912, a first-class cabin on *the Titanic* was the absolute pinnacle of luxury travel. But compare that with a typical balcony suite on a Carnival cruise ship today. The *Titanic* looked more ornate in an old-fashioned way, but a Carnival room is just as big and, by current standards, far more comfortable. The *Titanic* room at the time would have been within financial reach of only the wealthiest. Today, Carnival caters to the middle and upper middle class. In 2008 an expected 12.8 million people vacationed on cruise ships like Carnival's, staying in suites that rival the *Titanic*'s.[14] Cruise ships—even first-class cabins—by the 2000s had become mass-market enough that they were by no means a special luxury.

Tiffany, by the way, figured out the fallacy of its strategy. Worried about erosion of the brand, it conducted focus groups and customer research and found that the brand was becoming associated with inexpensive silver jewelry. One Tiffany customer, Barbara Graffeo, a New York apparel company owner in her mid-forties, said that she had a box full of Tiffany jewelry at home. "I don't wear them anymore because everyone wears them now," she said, summing up the problem. "You used to aspire to be able to buy something at Tiffany, but now it's not that special anymore."[15]

So Tiffany jacked up prices on its silver baubles to push them out of reach of the typical, mall-roaming teenage girl. At the same time, it recommitted to its upscale clientele, renovating stores to emphasize exclusive, high-priced jewelry. The company lost a ton of business at the lower end at first, but high-end sales slowly climbed back. Tiffany's stock dipped, wavered, then climbed in the late 2000s (until the 2008 financial crisis knocked down the shares of every retailer). By abandoning the fidelity mirage, Tiffany saved its brand.

PART THREE

The Trade-Off in Practice

CHAPTER NINE

Innovation

Irving Wladawsky-Berger grew up in pre-communist Cuba, the son of a Polish mother and Russian father who had moved to the island and opened a shop. After Fidel Castro came to power in 1959 the family fled to Chicago, where they had relatives. Irving was fifteen. He ended up attending the University of Chicago as an undergrad, excelled, and stayed on until he got a doctorate in physics. In 1970, IBM hired Wladawsky-Berger as a lab researcher; he thought he was going to spend his career as a scientist. A one-year sabbatical in marketing changed his mind. He found he had a knack for marrying technical concepts with business strategy. By 1985, Wladawsky-Berger rose to vice president in IBM's mainframe division. In 1996, CEO Lou Gerstner gave Wladawsky-Berger the critical job of conceiving and guiding IBM's overall Internet strategy.

While in that position, Wladawsky-Berger played a key role in the company's gutsy, much-publicized decision to embrace Linux—the free, open-source software developed by a community of unpaid software enthusiasts. IBM's move took tech watchers by surprise and seemed to defy logic. Yet it turned out to be brilliant, turning around IBM's fortunes in an important part of the computer market. To hear Wladawsky-Berger tell it, the decision was all about the role innovation plays in the fidelity/convenience tradeoff.

The Linux decision goes back to the late 1990s, when IBM ran into a problem in its business of making high-powered computers—often called servers—that run websites and other Internet-based offerings such as e-mail. IBM made some of the world's most powerful servers, and they ran on the most capable, rock-solid, big-computer operating system, dubbed AIX. But IBM was losing tons of business in this server market—particularly to Sun Microsystems computers, running on Sun's Solaris operating system. Sun's combination cost less and performed less well than an IBM machine running AIX, but was good enough for the required tasks. IBM was also increasingly losing business to Intel-based servers running Microsoft operating systems—which, again, were no match for the performance of AIX, but cost less and worked well enough for most Internet operations.

"IBM was so geared to high fidelity," Wladawsky-Berger told me.[1] "We tended to over-engineer and over-support products. AIX was the high-fidelity operating system. It was The Four Seasons. But not everybody can afford The Four Seasons."

IBM's typical reaction to competition was to add features, power, and cost, climbing higher up the fidelity axis. Sometimes that works. But in this case the tactic wasn't paying off. Sun and Microsoft had found a sweet spot on the fidelity/convenience equation for high-volume servers—just below IBM on fidelity, but a big jump to the right of IBM on convenience. In this particular market, IBM's push for fidelity using the AIX operating system was overkill. To customers who needed high-volume servers to process straightforward tasks, IBM, Sun, or Microsoft systems all could handle the job. So, from many a customer's perspective, the three were about tied on fidelity—since yet higher fidelity brought little added benefit. An IBM AIX system was like a super-high-end stereo system that puts out sounds the human ear can't hear.

When there's a tie on fidelity, the most convenient version of that fidelity wins. This works the other way, too—a convenience tie can be broken by the product or service that offers higher fidelity. In fact, it is the very essence of innovation and differentiation. If you and your competitor offer essentially the same product or service, but you can sell yours for less—you win. If you and your competitor offer a product or service that cost about the same and is just as easy to get, but yours is a little better—you win. But companies miss this point all the time. At IBM, management was so locked into its more-fidelity-is-better approach, it couldn't back off on fidelity and add a little convenience to compete against Sun and Microsoft in high-volume servers.

And still the decision to go with Linux was, at the time, wrenching for IBM. "We'd have been idiots if we didn't do it," Wladawsky-Berger said. "But businesses do a lot of idiotic things." Around the same time that AIX was being challenged, Wladawsky-Berger started paying attention to the blossoming Linux movement. Linux got its start with the Finnish programmer Linus Torvalds, who had the idea that millions of coders around the world working in their spare time could create, piece by piece, a viable computer operating system that might compete against AIX or Solaris or Windows. The Linux code got posted on the Internet, and anyone could work on it and improve on it— and then anyone could use it for free. The Linux open-source idea spawned thousands of other open-source projects in software and

media, including the Mozilla Firefox browser and the Wikipedia
online encyclopedia.

By the late 1990s, Linux was close to becoming good enough
to run high-volume servers—and it was free. If AIX couldn't
beat Solaris or Windows, how was it going to beat a free operating system? Sam Palmisano, at the time an IBM senior vice
president, came back from a global tour of Internet companies
and reported that he'd kept hearing about Linux from hot young
programmers. Wladawksy-Berger kept hearing about Linux, too.
IBM commissioned an internal study, which turned into a plan to
use Linux to undermine Sun and Microsoft. Wladawsky-Berger
and Palmisano got behind it, and helped convince CEO Gerstner.
Adopting Linux as IBM's operating system of choice looked like
a gigantic, risky, counterculture bet. But "Linux perfectly fit what
we needed," Wladawsky-Berger told me. "So we said, 'Screw it,
we're going for it—we'll embrace it.'"

In January 2000, IBM announced it was adopting Linux.
It would become Linux's biggest global benefactor, contributing programming code and technology to the Linux community
while forming a software-coding unit to work on making Linux
more robust for high-end corporate operations. At the announce-
ment, Wladawsky-Berger hedged his bets: "In all honesty, Linux
is all potential, and we'll have to see how it plays out," he told
reporters.

Linux quickly developed into server software that was good
enough to be considered alongside Solaris and Windows. So while
Sun sold a package of its server hardware and Solaris software at
a price that included both, IBM was able to offer IBM servers for
less because the Linux operating system came free. The fidelity
in servers offered by IBM, Sun and Microsoft was pretty much

equal. But now IBM had pulled a jujitsu move, flipping the server market on its head. IBM with AIX had been the least convenient; IBM with Linux became the most convenient. And in a fidelity tie, the product that is most convenient wins. By the early 2000s, Linux operating systems made up about one-third of all servers. In 2001, IBM announced its server market share had grown by 6.7 points. By 2004, IBM had a solid lead in server market share, with H-P coming in second and Sun third.

"Some competitor can always uncover a market just below your fidelity—at good-enough fidelity," Wladawsky-Berger said. "If they discover good-enough fidelity that's way down in cost, they'll kill you. It happens all the time. At IBM, it put pressure on us to either continue to differentiate by improving fidelity, or continuing to innovate to offer fidelity at lower prices—or exit that segment of business and move on. The question often becomes, 'Should we go up, down, or exit?'"

The best responses, Wladawsky-Berger told me, rely on innovation. Companies have to do something different to break the tie. IBM didn't invent Linux, but its innovation was the business decision to embrace a free, open-source operating system. That move put IBM in an entirely new position on the fidelity trade-off, and turned around its business in high-volume servers.

/ / /

Once in a while, a huge, sweeping innovation creates a strategic inflection point that entirely changes an industry. Digital cameras, as I discussed earlier, had that kind of impact on the consumer film industry. Personal computers did the same to the mainframe computer business. But such innovation is rare.

There is a more nuanced and common form of innovation that fits into the fidelity/convenience swap, and it's more like IBM's decision to embrace Linux, or the invention of a feature that gives an edge to an age-old product. Consider the Coors Light "cold activated" label. It's pretty hard to differentiate midprice beer. Coors thought it would try to add a little fidelity in 2008 by making a label that changes color when the beer inside gets cold. (Hard to know how big a role the added fidelity played in getting people to buy Coors Light instead of another beer, but Coors Light has become Coors's bestselling brand.)

Most companies are not the super-fidelity leader, or the super-convenience powerhouse. Nor are most companies hopelessly stuck in the depths of the fidelity belly; rather, they land somewhere between convenience and fidelity, while leaning more heavily in one direction than the other. Competitors tend to cluster around each other in the same area on a fidelity/convenience chart. To gain an edge, these companies have to decide whether to move up a notch in terms of fidelity or down a notch in terms of convenience. Some find imaginative ways to add features or quality for the same price, or keep pace with existing features and quality and drop the price. Small moves can bring small victories. Truly creative ideas, on the other hand, can change the dynamics of a market, as IBM did. This can happen in fast-changing industries such as computers, or in mature, seemingly static sectors—like vacuum cleaners.

Colin Angle never thought he'd be in the vacuum-cleaner business. As an undergrad at the Massachusetts Institute of Technology in 1988, he got involved with the university's famous Artificial Intelligence (AI) Lab, run by one of the foremost thinkers about robotics, Rodney Brooks. A couple of years later, Angle,

Brooks, and another student from the lab, Helen Greiner, started a company to design and sell commercial robots. They didn't yet know what those robots would do, but Angle said he kept getting hints. "I could bet that if I was introduced to someone who was not a techie, nearly every time they'd say, 'When are you going to make a robot to clean my floors?'" Angle told me.[2] Angle would smile and nod, while the company—eventually named iRobot—worked on robots that could find underwater mines and did other dangerous things for police and the military. Two projects changed the company's course. One was a partnership with S.C. Johnson to make a high-priced industrial floor-cleaning robot. The other was a deal with Hasbro to put artificial intelligence into a doll called My Real Baby—a partnership that taught iRobot about the challenges of low-cost manufacturing. Between the two, Angle started thinking about all those requests for a floor-cleaning consumer robot, and decided that iRobot should make a robot vacuum that cost $200.[3]

The price point was important. iRobot didn't want to make an expensive toy that happened to clean floors. It wanted to make a competitive vacuum cleaner that could clean floors by itself. In the vacuum-cleaner market in the 2000s, you'd find a cluster of simple models that cost around fifty or sixty dollars, and another cluster of more-robust models that cost $150 to $200. Vacuum makers also sold high-end models that cost as much as $1,500, but few people bought them. Angle wanted to compete against the robust models, matching their fidelity. In other words, he wanted his $200 robot vacuum to clean floors just as well as a $200 traditional vacuum.

For decades, the cluster of $150-to-$200 vacuums jostled with each other in a rather small range of the sector's fidelity/

convenience trade-off. Some lowered prices a bit to compete on convenience. Others added an extra nozzle here or a control there to differentiate on fidelity. But you didn't find many bold leaps in the vacuum-cleaner space. Most people who had a fifteen-year-old vacuum didn't feel like they were missing much.

There's an old cliché in business that people don't buy a quarter-inch drill—they buy a quarter-inch hole. The drill happens to be the best means to an end, but if there were a better means, people would buy it. They don't give a hoot about the drill. They want the hole it makes. The same kind of saying can apply to vacuum cleaners. People don't buy a vacuum cleaner—they buy a clean floor. But for decades the only way to get a clean floor had been to push a vacuum cleaner over it.

In the fall of 2002, iRobot introduced the Roomba vacuum cleaner. For the first time in ages, someone had come up with an innovative leap in how to get a clean floor—a leap in convenience. The round, low Roomba looked more like a cross between a bathroom scale and a Belgian waffle iron than a traditional vacuum. It came armed with a computer, sensors, and AI (artificial intelligence) that could help it figure out the size and shape of a room and how to make sure every inch got cleaned. It worked entirely on its own—you'd set the Roomba down on a floor, turn it on, and it would beep and whir and do the vacuuming job with no human intervention. In marketing campaigns, the company talked up Roomba's suction power and array of tiny brushes, claiming it would do as good a job as any vacuum in its price range. IRobot was trying to enter the $200 vacuum-cleaner market at about the same fidelity as its competitors, but with a significant jump in convenience. Buy a Roomba, the pitch went, and you'll get the same clean floor in a much easier way for the same cost.

That 2002 holiday season—while the economy was muted by the tech bust and the September 11, 2001, terrorist attacks—Roomba took off. Within two years, iRobot sold 2 million Roomba vacuums.[4] That's from a standing start, with no experience selling to retailers, no distribution channel, and zero brand recognition. iRobot brought an innovation in convenience into a mature sector, and used it to win customers from the cluster of competitors.

iRobot plans to develop robots to do other kinds of housework. "If we can get that magical value-versus-cost equation as good or better than the current situation, we will build that product," Angle said. "We believe there are many tasks within the home that are ripe for automation." iRobot's formula going forward is to match conventional products on fidelity and cost, and then use robotics to gain the upper hand in convenience.

/ / /

On a bright spring day, I stopped into the headquarters of Idealab in Pasadena, California, to talk with founder and CEO Bill Gross. He is a small, kind of nerdy individual, the sort who might be played by Rick Moranis in a movie. His office is a little cubicle tucked into the middle of Idealab's semi-open, warehouse-like layout. His orange plastic bookshelves are jammed with gadgets and half-finished prototype parts fresh out of Idealab's machine shop. Idealab acts as a well-oiled tech company incubator. It helps start companies, houses them, helps them get going, then spins them out. Past spinouts have included NetZero, Citysearch, and eToys. But the Idealab company Gross most wanted to talk about the day I arrived is called eSolar. In April 2007, eSolar got $130 million in funding from Google.org (Google's philanthropic arm) and other investors.

eSolar developed a way to dramatically drive down the cost of producing solar energy on a large scale. This is not about solar panels on a home's roof. It's about replacing entire coal or natural gas power plants with solar plants. Until eSolar came along, the few solar power plants were giant civil engineering projects, requiring the construction of dozens of barn-size parabolic mirrors mounted on concrete poles sunk twenty feet into the ground, precisely aimed at a power-generating tower. The sun would reflect off the mirrors and focus on water pipes in the tower, and the intense heat would turn the water to steam and drive a turbine, which would generate electricity. These projects cost so much to build, they made no economic sense without significant government subsidies. The solar plants certainly weren't economically competitive with power plants that burned coal.

Gross's eSolar, though, figured there was a way to use computer technology to run solar plants better. Instead of relying on dozens of gigantic mirrors, eSolar uses thousands of smaller mirrors, each the size of a refrigerator door and mounted on a metal frame controlled by a small motor. The mirrors are scattered around the tower, placed on the ground. Digital cameras at the site track the sun and feed that information to a computer, which in turn moves the mirror motors to angle each mirror so it collects the most sun and fires it at the steam-producing pipes. As of this writing, the first plant was being built—and Gross was pretty certain that it would not only work, but would allow solar plants to be built at a fraction of the cost of current solar plants. "The goal is to be cheaper than a coal plant," Gross told me. It's an audacious goal, but it would allow solar to replace coal plants. Imagine having an economically competitive alternative to the coal power plants that spew carbon into the atmosphere and contribute mightily to global warming. "The only way to save the world is if you get solar cheaper than coal," Gross said dramatically.

Now, consumers don't buy power plants—they buy electricity. And electricity is an interesting product. "It's just electrons," Gross said. "It's the ultimate commodity. There is no fidelity!" There's no such thing as better-quality electricity, or electricity with more features. All electricity works the same. So for nearly 100 years, the only thing that mattered to consumers about electricity was convenience. And once electricity was pretty consistently available everywhere, the only factor in convenience was cost. The only way to differentiate electricity has been to offer it cheaper.

Here, though, is Gross's interesting insight. These days, because of concerns about global warming, a utility could gain a fidelity advantage if a greater percentage of its power was generated using renewable resources. An increasing number of consumers will think better of the electricity that comes from a solar plant. eSolar stands a chance of making a dent in the electricity market by matching competitors on convenience, but taking a step up in fidelity.

/ / /

Business bookshelves are filled with titles about innovation, and often they're about how companies can come up with cool new ideas. The fidelity swap is a way to put those ideas in context and see what they might do for a product or service in an overall marketplace.

The fidelity swap can also help a company see why and how competitors are putting on pressure, and facilitate ideas about how to respond. Is the competitive pressure coming from the convenience side or the fidelity side? And what is the best response? Do you fight convenience with even greater convenience? Or by moving up in fidelity? The answer can vary depending on the brand, the industry, and surrounding conditions. Analyzing the fidelity/convenience trade-offs can help tease out options.

In the 1980s, American Airlines executed a brilliant fidelity trade-off response to People Express. It was so good, it drove People Express right out of business.

I remember People Express fondly. The airline started operations in 1981 at Newark International Airport, and I was in college at Rutgers, about twenty minutes away down Route 1. The traveling public had never seen anything like People Express. Fares were almost as cheap as taking a Greyhound bus. For a while, flights between Newark and Washington, D.C., cost $19 each way. The airline was religiously no-frills, but customers were so giddy about the unheard-of low fares, they bought into the austerity. It became part of the fun. And People Express turned into a nightmare for the major airlines.

Before 1978, the airline industry and its fares were regulated by the federal government. The airlines rarely competed on price, so their cultures were geared toward competing for customers based on fidelity. A 1977 TWA commercial, for instance, used the tag line "It's built for comfort," and touted a steak dinner in coach on coast-to-coast flights. In the 1970s, United tried putting a "Friendship Lounge" for socializing in the coach section of DC-10s. Rarely did ads mention ticket prices.

Donald Burr had been president at Texas International Airlines in that era. Once the Carter administration ended airline regulation in 1978, Burr saw an opening to compete on convenience, and quit Texas Air. He leased seventeen Boeing 737-100s and space in an abandoned warehouse at Newark Airport's north terminal. People Express had no computerized reservation systems, no meals, no first class, and no on-board movies. It kept unions out and salaries down. It cost People Express just 5.28 cents to fly a passenger one mile. The cost for airlines in the rest of the industry was more like 8.6 cents. The gap was so huge, People Express could charge ridiculously low prices that competitors could not touch. Travelers poured into People Express planes. Within four years of launch, the airline was the fifth-largest in the United States, serving 107 cities—including London and Brussels. In 1985 it brought in $1 billion in revenue—at the time, the fastest company ever to get to $1 billion in revenue.[5]

Major U.S. airlines in the late 1970s competed in a fidelity cluster, none much more convenient or higher fidelity than all the rest. They maneuvered in small ways—like adding the steak dinner—that brought small payoffs. But then People Express came along. It took a couple of steps backward on fidelity, but leaped ahead in convenience while offering good-enough fidelity. People Express increasingly siphoned off fliers from the major carriers.

In American Airlines' Dallas headquarters, CEO Robert Crandall fumed—especially once People Express started flying to his home city. Crandall wanted his customers back. If he had considered American's options through a fidelity/convenience lens, he would have seen that one option would have been to fight convenience with convenience—perhaps by starting a separate low-cost, low-fidelity, low-fare airline that could go head-to-head with People. (That's a strategy United adopted in the 1990s, starting Ted to compete against low-cost carriers such as Southwest.) He might have decided to bump up American's fidelity, get out of serving low-end leisure fliers, and focus on winning just business travelers and others who would pay high fares for better service. Either might have worked. But instead, Crandall opted for a more devastating and innovative strategy. He set out to get close to People Express on convenience, while bludgeoning it on fidelity.

Crandall's innovation was to invest in nascent technology called yield management. Computer scientists were just figuring out how to write software that could analyze historical data about ticket prices and load factors on every route, and make predictions about how to fill planes with a range of customers from business travelers to college students scrimping to fly home for a weekend. This gave birth to the now-familiar way tickets get sold—low fares if you buy weeks in advance and stay over a weekend; high fares if you buy soon before a flight and come back the next day. The low fare for a cross-country seat might match or even beat a discount airline's fare, while the high fare would be four or five times that amount. American's yield-management system would figure out how to set those prices so the airline could operate at its higher cost structure, continue to offer major-airline benefits like meals and movies, and still make a healthy profit.[6]

By 1985, American had the system in high gear, and it worked as Crandall imagined. To fliers looking for a low-cost fare, American suddenly looked as convenient as People Express—but American had a lot more fidelity. So consumers increasingly chose American. But because American wasn't giving up any fidelity— which would have been the case had it started a separate low-cost carrier—it could still lure the kinds of travelers who would pay hefty ticket prices.

People Express couldn't respond. Its ticket prices were already about as low as they could go. It didn't have the higher fares that might have given the company the money to add fidelity. In 1996, a decade after People Express was forced into bankruptcy, Burr described what happened. "We were a vibrant, profitable company from 1981 to 1985, and then we tipped right over into losing $50 million a month," Burr said. "We were still the same company. What changed was American's ability to do widespread yield management in every one of our markets. We had been profitable from the day we started until American came at us with Ultimate Super Savers. That was the end of our run because they were able to underprice us at will and surreptitiously. There was nothing left to defend us."[7]

Crandall innovated like a maestro with the principles of the fidelity/convenience trade-off, and won.

CHAPTER TEN

Disasters

In February 1994, at the spectacular seaside Pebble Beach golf course near Monterey, California, pro golfers such as Tom Watson and Johnny Miller mixed with CEOS and celebrities. The occasion was the AT&T Pebble Beach National Pro-Am. AT&T's CEO, Robert Allen, was there, and Microsoft CEO Bill Gates was on hand as a guest. Gates had recently proposed to Allen that AT&T and Microsoft form an alliance. The proposal set off a furious debate inside AT&T about the wisdom of getting into bed with Microsoft, which at the time wielded more power than perhaps any other company in the technology world—and had a reputation for brutal tactics. Gates and Allen were at a standoff, and an intermediary, Craig McCaw, the Seattle-based billionaire who built the first nationwide cell-phone system and sold it to AT&T, tried to get them to talk it through.

"I was telling them they were both acting unreasonable— like big not-invented-here companies," McCaw told me. The talks went nowhere that day—and no alliance would ever come of them. But at one point during the Pro-Am, McCaw pulled Gates aside for a private conversation. "I told Bill, 'I've got an idea and

I want you to come in with me—just close your eyes and jump,'"
McCaw said. "To his credit, he did jump."[1]

Gates leaped into what would become one of the biggest fi-
ascos in technology history. The venture was called Teledesic—
an outrageous attempt to put 840 satellites into orbit to form a
global wireless broadband Internet system. Ultimately, Teledesic
would endure a slow death before even the first satellite went up
into space.

How could two wildly successful tech visionaries—Gates and
McCaw—misfire so badly? They each put in $5 million of their
own money. Boeing invested $100 million. Saudi prince Alwa-
leed Bin Talal put in $200 million. Motorola joined in, contribut-
ing technology and contracting work. Lockheed Martin signed
on to do the launches.

The origins of Teledesic can be traced to Ed Tuck, an entrepreneur who started the Magellan global positioning satellite
company. Tuck borrowed some ideas from President Reagan's
"Star Wars" Strategic Defense Initiative, and developed a plan to
surround the earth with a constellation of low-orbiting satellites,
each one acting like a switch on a network. The plan called for
840 satellites (eventually down-shifted to 288). It would cost, at a
minimum, $9 billion (critics suggested Teledesic would cost more
than double that amount). In 1990, McCaw decided he liked the
idea and bought in, at first secretly funding Tuck's research and
development. A month or so after the 1994 Pebble Beach conversation with Gates, Teledesic filed documents with the Federal
Communications Commission. When the documents became
public, the news of Teledesic broke and made newspaper front
pages everywhere. The intense scrutiny took McCaw and Gates
by surprise. McCaw told me that he thought the media liked the

story because it could be spun as "two spoiled rich kids who had finally gone over the edge."

McCaw and Gates had plenty of reasons to think Teledesic would work. In 1994 the Internet was barely a blip on the public's radar. Gates's 1995 bestselling book *The Road Ahead* only mentions the Internet a couple of times in passing. McCaw and Gates believed Teledesic was way ahead of the curve—a vital new stage of what was then often referred to as the "information superhighway." Early Teledesic documents noted that "half the world's population lives more than two hours from a telephone," yet an era was dawning when not just voice, but data and video communication, would be essential. U.S. phone companies still had copper lines running to neighborhoods and homes, and those systems couldn't handle high-speed data. Cable systems couldn't yet carry two-way communications, either. Communications systems were even worse in most of the rest of the world, especially Asia and the former Soviet bloc. Cellular networks were in their infancy, still relying on slow-moving analog signals. Add it up, and Teledesic in 1994 looked as if it had an opening to become a powerful global Internet provider. All it had to do was meet its plan to start service in 2002.

From comments he made to me in the late 1990s, it was obvious McCaw knew Teledesic was a major gamble. "It's outlandish enough that you've got to figure not a lot of people are going to copy you," he said then. "It has the protection of insanity."

As a communications system, Teledesic in 1994 started out deep in the fidelity belly—for eight years, according to its own plan, the system would not exist. It was going to take that long to get Teledesic up and running; the system would not work at all until the whole thing was in place. Teledesic would remain in one static spot in the realm of fidelity/convenience trade-offs for *eight years*—which, in technology, is several lifetimes.

During those eight years, the tech effect would continue to push the boundaries of fidelity and convenience outward. Teledesic in 1994 aimed at what it thought was a high-fidelity and high-convenience position. By 2002 that spot certainly would be overtaken, possibly by technology that hadn't even been invented in 1994. Teledesic might have seemed like a cool and desirable technology when it was conceived, but the success of a product or service isn't about how it performs in absolute terms—it's about how it performs in relation to its competitors. If communications technologies hadn't changed since 1994, Teledesic might have gotten built and been a huge hit. But they did change, *radically,* making Teledesic obsolete and unnecessary before it ever (literally) got off the ground. Teledesic ignored the tech effect, with disastrous consequences.

A second observation about Teledesic and the fidelity/convenience trade-off: the 1994 documents show that Teledesic was chasing a fidelity mirage right out of the box.[2] The company thought it could provide high-speed Internet that would trump the speed and reliability of any wired network, making Teledesic the highest-fidelity Internet provider. It also thought it could be the most convenient service—the one network available absolutely anywhere at competitive prices. But, as discussed earlier, pursuing both fidelity and convenience is a fool's errand. If Teledesic tried to stay ahead of the highest-speed Internet services and remain a high-fidelity choice, the company would have to invest so much money in updating satellites, it couldn't possibly offer cheap service for a mass global market.

All of that seems easy to see in hindsight. But would it have been so easy to tease it out at the time? Such analysis wouldn't have required knowing precisely *how* communications technology would evolve—it just required knowing that over a span of eight years, it most certainly *would* evolve. That is why chasing the fidelity mirage is such a flawed idea. If Teledesic had aimed at super-convenience from the start, it might have tried to design a low-cost global system focused on delivering cheap, good-enough service to a broad swath of people who couldn't get or didn't want to pay for premium services. Teledesic might have become a communications global Wal-Mart. Instead, by reaching for both fidelity and convenience, Teledesic was destined to offer a service that was neither fish nor fowl—neither loved nor needed.

So what did happen to Teledesic? The short answer is that it just fizzled out. As technology and market projections changed, Teledesic's engineers tried to compensate by redesigning the system, switching contractors, and looking at ways to build Teledesic on top of existing satellite systems. When Motorola's Iridium—another audacious satellite project conceived at about the same time as Teledesic—filed for bankruptcy in August 1999, investors decided not to put any more money into Teledesic. By the fall of 2002—when it was supposed to start serving customers—Teledesic was stalled, and starved for cash. It suspended all satellite work and shut down.

/ / /

Most companies at some point make a product or offer a service that lands with a thud. IBM tried to sell the public on its PCjr, Coca-Cola blundered into New Coke, Sony developed Betamax, and Ford made the legendary Edsel automobile. No management model, elaborate algorithm, or new way of thinking is going to eliminate poor decisions. But the fidelity swap can help businesses evaluate potential products or investments in the context of competition, changing technology, and the choices customers will likely make. It can help a CEO, entrepreneur, or managerial team spot a calamity waiting to happen.

When I apply the fidelity swap to the business disasters I've reported on and know well, a handful of points pop out. If you're considering whether to bet on a certain product, first decide on the bucket that product belongs in. In other words, create a fidelity/convenience trade-off chart, and try to understand where the new product would fit in. Here are a few things to consider:

- Don't forget the tech effect. The outer borders of fidelity and convenience constantly move outward, driven by evolving technology. Wherever a product or service lands on the fidelity-or-convenience axis today, it will be in a different position tomorrow. This is one reason time-to-market is so crucial. The longer a product or service trudges through development, the more the borders move before the product lands on the market. Google beats the tech effect by throwing "beta" versions of new products on the market as quickly as possible, then tweaking them to keep up with changing technology. Of course, that approach won't work for everything. Airbus needed eleven years to develop and build the A380 super-jumbo airliner, which began to go into service in the late 2000s. Airbus had to hope that the A380 was such a leap up the fidelity axis that it would still be a breakthrough product despite the tech effect. (It helped that the tech effect moves slowly in the air transport industry, compared with the fast pace of the Web.)

• Success is not about whether a product is cool or hip—it's about where the product falls amid fidelity/convenience trade-offs. This is where a lot of companies falter. They make something that is very gee-whiz. They try it out on friends or focus groups who pronounce it amazing. But in the broader market, the key is whether it will beat competitors on convenience or fidelity. Think of General Magic's gizmos in the mid-1990s, or Amazon.com's Kindle now. Both are great technological achievements and undeniably cool products. But on a fidelity/convenience chart, General Magic was stuck in the belly. The Kindle started out there, and Amazon is trying to find a path out.

• Different sets of consumers make different fidelity/convenience trade-offs. Technology that a younger generation finds convenient, an older generation might find inconvenient. To early adopters, the fact that a product is new and amazing pumps up its aura—which gives the product great fidelity to that group, but does little to entice the broader market. Never evaluate a product or service based on the enthusiasm of early adopters.

• Starting small gives a product or service agility, so it can adjust in response to the tech effect and competitors. Projects that start huge—Teledesic, Iridium, Webvan—have a difficult time adjusting to changing conditions or technology. Products and services that take years to develop are huge gambles because it's so difficult to guess how the tech effect will play out years from now.

• New technologies almost always start out inside the fidelity belly. The ones that make it out are the ones that clearly aim at either high fidelity or high convenience. Aiming at both is a bad idea.

/ / /

The fidelity swap might have provided some early clues about the expectations for one of the coolest, most gee-whiz products of the past decade: the Segway scooter.

Dean Kamen was a child prodigy tinkerer. Born in 1951 on Long Island, Kamen was making controllers for sound and light systems in his parents' basement by middle school. The hobby turned into a side business by high school, and then Kamen won a contract with New York's Hayden Planetarium and was asked to automate the New Year's Eve ball drop on Times Square. He got kicked out of Worcester Polytechnic Institute because he worked on his own projects instead of those of his class. Once out on his own, he focused his energy on medical devices. Early on, he created the Auto-Syringe, a portable infusion pump that for the first time could administer a steady dose of drugs without the patient having to stay in a hospital. Kamen's lab, DEKA Research and Development, invented ever more sophisticated medical gadgets, culminating in the late 1990s with the Ibot—a six-wheeled "human transporter" for the wheelchair-bound. The $20,000 Ibot was crammed with technology that would let the chair climb stairs and rise up on two wheels to the height of a standing person, maintaining better balance than someone standing on his own two legs. By that point, Kamen had fans and followers from the U.S. Department of Defense to the West Coast's technology community.[3] The Ibot had won Kamen a reputation for doing the near impossible.

The Ibot's balancing system turned Kamen in a new direction. While still perfecting the Ibot, Kamen started a secret project, code-named Ginger, and shared his plans with a small circle of Silicon Valley's elite. Among them were the superstar venture capitalist John Doerr (who had backed Netscape, Amazon.com, and other giant tech hits), Amazon CEO Jeff Bezos, and Apple Computers' Steve Jobs. Doerr and Bezos invested in a separate company Kamen was forming to build this new thing. As rumors about Ginger leaked during 2001, Doerr predicted the company would get to $1 billion in sales faster than any startup in history. Jobs remarked to the press that Kamen's invention would be bigger than the personal computer.[4]

When Kamen unveiled Ginger—officially branded with the name Segway—in December 2001, it got worldwide media coverage. Everyone saw that the Segway was, basically, an extraordinary powered scooter. The Segway's most compelling feature was the balancing and steering system, which let the user drive the thing by slightly shifting weight. The public was fascinated. Meanwhile, Kamen predicted his Segway would replace cars in urban areas and transform the way cities are designed. He told the media that the Segway would be to the car what the car was to the horse and buggy. He built a factory in New Hampshire that could make 40,000 Segways a month.

But there were barriers to the Segway's acceptance. The machines cost more than $3,000 each. They moved too fast to use on sidewalks, but too slowly to mix with traffic. A Segway offered no place to carry a few bags of groceries or bring along your child. There was the question of where to park one, or if it was okay to bring a Segway into a building. Segways seemed less like practical, everyday transportation than like a pretty expensive toy.

If Kamen had considered the fidelity/convenience trade-off, he might have tried fitting the Segway in different buckets. The most obvious, considering his thoughts about the Segway and cities, would have been "urban transportation." The super-convenient urban transportation is walking. It's cheap and always available. And the high-fidelity transportation is cars—expensive to own and park, but private, protected from weather, and they help to give you a sense of identity. Taxis offer a little less fidelity than cars, but are a little more convenient. Subways, buses, bikes, and skateboards all have their places on a fidelity chart.

Where would the Segway land? Well, it's not very convenient, since it costs a lot and can't always be used on sidewalks or roads. The Segway offers some fidelity, but the first time you had to ride a Segway in the rain carrying groceries, you'd decide the fidelity didn't come anywhere near that of a taxi or your own car. So, on an "urban transportation" chart, the Segway would land squarely inside the belly. And the Segway doesn't seem to have a path out. The Segway can't move up in fidelity to compete with cars, unless a covered version with a trunk is developed. (In 2009, Segway and General Motors unveiled a prototype two-seater Segway called PUMA.) If Kamen could make a Segway that costs $300 instead of $3,000, the scooters might become convenient enough to spread to a mass market—but Kamen has never indicated he intends to go that route.

While the Segway is undeniably cool, in the context of personal urban transportation, it is practically irrelevant. A certain set of wealthy, tech-driven consumers were ecstatic about the Segway. But they were classic early adopters. The Segway did not start small, growing out of a need, adjusting to changing conditions and technologies over time. It landed on the market after years of development, fully formed and attempting to create a need. The general public found it did not need the Segway, and it did not love the Segway enough to pay $3,000. And the Segway had no way to migrate to either need or love.

The Segway found a home in a few niche commercial markets. Product pickers in Amazon's vast warehouses ride Segways, and so do some police in New York's Central Park. Otherwise, Segways are primarily toys for people with a lot of disposable income. Apple cofounder Steve Wozniak famously started a Segway polo league in Silicon Valley.

Kamen has not revealed the number of Segways sold, but in the fall of 2006, nearly five years after the Segway was unveiled, the company issued a recall for all the Segways out there. The total was 23,500.[5] The company as of this writing was still operating and trying to sell into more niche markets, including city tour operators and airport security. But the Segway factory isn't making 40,000 a month or even 40,000 a year, much less revolutionizing cities.

/ / /

Why did the Apple Newton crash and the Palm Pilot succeed?

Those early handheld computers were introduced about three years apart. A multibillion-dollar corporation with a stellar, beloved brand created the Newton. The Palm Pilot got its start from a desperate entrepreneur who was running out of money. The Newton turned into a legendary embarrassment for Apple. The Palm was a breakthrough hit. How did this happen? And what does it look like through the lens of the fidelity/convenience trade-off?

I went to the unveiling of the Newton in August 1993. Apple rented Boston's vast, ornate Symphony Hall. Executives and journalists from all over the world packed the place. The media had worked itself into a frenzy of anticipation for the little computer. At the event, Gareth Powell, a publisher of Australian computer magazines, gushed to me, "This is going to change the world, I'm sure of it."[6]

The idea of the "personal digital assistant"—or PDA—had been seeping into the public's consciousness for a few years. PDAs were the first attempts to squeeze serious computing power into a device that could easily be carried around. Cell phones at the time were nothing more than phones for voice calls. PDAs stirred a feeling that science fiction was coming to life. A computer in your pocket was a truly amazing concept. And lots of companies took a shot at the technology. AT&T tried to market a PDA with a cell phone attached, called the EO. It wasn't exactly portable—given that it was the size of a cereal box and as heavy as a hardcover copy of *War and Peace*. Japan's Casio built the Zoomer, which was smaller but never worked all that well. The world stood ready for a PDA that met the hype.

Apple started talking about the Newton in January 1992, when CEO John Sculley gave a keynote speech at the Consumer Electronics show. The Newton that Apple unveiled in Boston more than eighteen months later was the size of a paperback book, with a gray-scale touch screen and a plastic stylus. The software was supposed to recognize handwriting and turn it into text, although it frustrated most users and rarely correctly recognized any writing. The Newton otherwise didn't do much. It could connect to a computer or a network, but that was very difficult to do. The Newton was essentially an isolated device. It had a calendar, address book, and notepad, but little else built in. And it cost from $699 to $1,500.

I remember playing with a Newton for about twenty minutes at the Boston event, and feeling rather underwhelmed. I asked Apple to send me a Newton I could test, but the company was so worried about bad reviews, it said I'd first have to fly to Apple headquarters in Cupertino, California, and attend a Newton class. If you have to make people go to a class to learn to use a device, you're already in trouble.[7]

And, in fact, the Newton tanked. The public found it disappointing. It was too big, cost too much, and didn't do enough. The killer was the handwriting recognition. The Newton's failure helped drive Sculley out of Apple. He stepped down as CEO in June 1993, a couple of months before Newton's unveiling, but remained as chairman. In October 1993, he was pushed out of the chairman position, too. In 1998, Apple killed the Newton.

Through the lens of the fidelity swap, the Newton of 1993 never stood a chance. The fidelity/convenience chart for the Newton's market might have been described as "personal information management"—calendars, notes, addresses, e-mails, to-do lists, household budgets, and so on. The Newton wasn't enough of a computer to be a computer, and it didn't have the communications capabilities to be anything like the BlackBerry of later years. It was, really, a glorified notepad. And in that realm, the super-convenient solution was paper and a pen. Super-fidelity would have been a laptop computer. For the broad market, the Newton fell into the fidelity belly—inconvenient compared to paper, not very capable compared to a laptop. Most people could find no reason to buy a Newton. And Apple never found a way to migrate Newton out toward fidelity or convenience. So Newton died, smearing Apple's reputation for years.

The Newton's failure nearly doomed a little company called Palm Computing. Engineering whiz Jeff Hawkins and business-woman Donna Dubinsky formed Palm in 1992 to make software for PDAs, thinking the category was about to take off. After the Newton, the whole category seemed like a lost cause. "Everyone thought that after all the failures, this was just the wrong place to be," Hawkins told me on Palm's tenth anniversary. "No one wanted to work with us."[8]

Around 1994, with Palm on the ropes, Hawkins and Dubinsky had a meeting with Bruce Dunlevie, a young venture capitalist who had funded Palm. "We were sitting in his office," Hawkins said. "Donna was saying people don't want to work with us anymore, blah blah blah, and we can't raise money, blah blah blah—and Bruce said, 'Look, do you know what product you would build if you could build the right product?' And I remember saying, 'Yeah.' Even though I hadn't really thought about it. So I kind of lied."

Much to Hawkins's surprise, Dunlevie said that's exactly what Palm should do—build its own device. "I said, 'Bruce, that would require us doing the hardware and the software and the operating system and marketing it,'" Hawkins recalled. "And by the way, we had $3 million in the bank and twenty-seven employees of which only one person had any hardware experience, and that was me. And I said, 'Boy, it's real hard to do that.' And Bruce said, 'Well, what else are you going to do? You could bleed and die a slow death.' So I said, 'Well, that's great. We'll go do it. If you say it's okay, we'll go do it.'"

As Hawkins was saying that, Dubinsky was thinking about numbers. "We actually had enough money to develop the product," she told me. "But we didn't have enough to put it into manufacturing."

The strange thing is that even though Hawkins wasn't aware of it, he really did know exactly what kind of handheld computer stood a chance of succeeding. It was all in his head. He'd watched the other handhelds sink, and had learned from their mistakes. The night of that Dunlevie meeting, Hawkins went home and mapped out the Palm Pilot in one sitting. He showed it to his board and other investors, who proclaimed the project—to use Hawkins's word—"nutzo." Still, Hawkins persisted, working with another Palm executive, Ed Colligan, to develop and build the Pilot. In February 1996, they tentatively showed their device at a major tech industry conference called DEMO—and were amazed when the crowd loved it. "The moment felt like, wow, this is going to work," Dubinsky said. "People are going to buy it."

What did Palm get right that Apple got so wrong? There were four key differences between the Pilot and the Newton, and together they put the Pilot in a completely different place in the fidelity swap.

Most significantly, Hawkins had already been working on Graffiti—a funky writing method that got around the limitations of the day's handwriting-recognition technology—and used it in the Pilot. Simple strokes of the pen on the touch-sensitive part of the Pilot's screen represented certain letters. Graffiti required a bit of a learning curve for users, but at least it provided a usable way to enter text into the Palm. Another significant advance was the Pilot's simple way to synchronize with a PC: pop the Pilot into a cradle, push one button, and the Pilot and PC would exchange information, updating calendars and documents in both.

The other two important changes: the Palm Pilot was smaller than a Newton and could fit in a pocket or purse, and it cost less, starting at about $300.

Graffiti, the cradle, and the size all improved the experience of a personal digital assistant. Before the Pilot, PDAs were generally frustrating. The Pilot was a satisfying experience, particularly for tech-savvy users. It also quickly gained an aura as a cool new product—pulling a Palm device out at an airline gate announced that you were smart and hip and out in front of the tech trends. The fidelity of a Palm Pilot wasn't comparable with a full-scale laptop computer when it came to organizing personal information, but the fidelity was good enough and the convenience was better than a laptop—since a Pilot could ride in a pocket, ran on a couple of AAA batteries, and cost a fraction of the price of a laptop. The combination made the Pilot the first PDA to win a sustainable audience beyond early adopters.

In an odd twist, in the late 2000s Apple buried its Newton past when it developed the iPhone, emerging as the most exciting maker of personal devices. Meanwhile, the Palm brand struggled. Early disasters aren't necessarily disasters forever, and early victories don't guarantee long-term success.

/ / /

Tesla Motors is trying to help electric cars break out in the marketplace by making the first high-fidelity electric car. Shai Agassi is on a different quest. He believes his company, Better Place, can make electric cars more convenient than gas-powered cars and win the broad mass market.

It's a bold, idealistic, world-changing plan. By late 2008, Better Place had attracted $200 million in investment. Now it has to avoid becoming the next Teledesic.

Agassi grew up in Israel; he built a software company that he eventually sold to German software giant SAP for $400 million.

Dynamic and restless, Agassi worked for SAP for a couple of years, but in the mid-2000s started focusing on the problem of climate change. In 2007, at the age of forty, Agassi left SAP to try to disrupt the global auto and oil industries.

His plan revolves around reimagining the car industry's business model. He wants to create an electric-car industry that operates somewhat along the lines of the U.S. mobile phone industry. AT&T Wireless, for example, subsidizes the price of cell phones made by Nokia, Samsung, and the like. Customers can get a free or deeply discounted phone when they sign up for AT&T's service; AT&T Wireless makes its money by selling airtime on its network. In Agassi's vision of the electric-car industry, Better Place would build a network of ways to recharge an electric car, including stations where a customer could pull in and have an empty battery swapped for a full one in a matter of minutes. Cars would be subsidized like cell phones—electric cars, whether they were made by Ford, Toyota, Tata, or any other company, would all use a standard, swappable Better Place battery. Better Place would underwrite the cost so that consumers could buy these cars for less than the cost of gas-powered cars. Then Better Place would charge for an electric car's equivalent of cell-phone airtime: the amount of power used, which roughly translates into miles driven.[9]

In a Better Place world, you'd buy a car of your choice and a monthly package—say, 1,000 miles a month. At home, you'd plug the car in to recharge it. If you're out driving and the battery charge gets near depleted, you'd pull into a Better Place station, and have the battery exchanged for a fully charged one for free. Software in Better Place's system would keep track of the amount of power you used and add it to your bill. If Better Place can offer consumers a cheaper car, and sell a package of miles for less than it would cost to buy gas to drive the same number of miles, the mass market will stampede to Better Place, Agassi reasons. Add in people's growing desire to clean up the environment, and Better Place would seem to be a sure-fire hit.

"The best way to do this is to build an open platform," Agassi said when I saw him interviewed on stage at a technology conference in 2008. "We build the platform, and the car companies build the applications—the cars."[10]

Agassi has won support from the government of Israel, which wants the nation to be a proving ground for Better Place. Idan Ofer, one of Israel's wealthiest men, committed $130 million to Agassi's company. Morgan Stanley and a couple of venture firms put up another $30 million. Renault started developing a Better Place–compatible car that's supposed to be ready by 2011. Agassi's plan seems to be coming together.

But here's where the fidelity-swap model comes into play. Like Teledesic, Better Place needs to put a massive, complex system into place before it can welcome its first customer. Better Place won't be a viable transportation option until motorists can be confident they can get their car batteries swapped and recharged anywhere they drive. At the same time, car companies won't invest in building Better Place cars unless they are confident the network is going to get built, and that consumers will want to purchase the cars. Better Place is shooting to land just beyond the convenience of gas-powered cars. To achieve that, its cars and fuel will have to be a little bit cheaper and at least as easy to get as today's gas-powered cars. The whole ecosystem has to come together, or it will never catch on.

Agassi acknowledges that building that ecosystem will be a

gigantic task. "We represent the biggest infrastructure project in the world," he told the tech conference audience. When asked by the interviewer how long that would take, Agassi evaded the question. But if the first Renault/Better Place car won't make it to the market until 2011, Better Place won't come together until years after that.

Like Teledesic, Better Place has to aim for a spot on the fidelity/convenience chart based on what the company thinks things will be like five or ten years out. In that time, the tech effect will keep moving the boundaries of convenience and fidelity. Better Place says it wants to be the super-convenient option for personal transportation. But by the time Better Place is up and running, that super-convenient spot might get overtaken by something else. Better Place can't start small and migrate and adjust with the tech effect—it's starting as a fully formed concept that pretty much has to either completely succeed or completely fail.

Teledesic didn't anticipate the fast rise of a global patchwork of ground-based, high-speed wireless networks. Similarly, there's no telling what might usurp Better Place's position on a fidelity/convenience chart in a decade. A breakthrough in fuel-cell battery technology, for example, could let an electric car drive for 500 miles between charges, minimizing the need for swappable batteries. Super-efficient hybrid gas engines might corner that market. A company called Aptera has made a gas car that gets 300 miles per gallon. Meanwhile, BMW is experimenting with hydrogen-powered cars. Could that technology leap into the super-convenient slot where Better Place hopes to land?

The fidelity/convenience trade-off throws light on the kind of bet Agassi is making—and the difficulty of pulling it off.

In mid-2008, Daimler Benz CEO Dieter Zetsche said his

company plans to start selling an electric Mercedes and electric Smart Car by 2010. He noted that Daimler was considering making batteries that could be leased and swapped out—a version of the Better Place concept. Even if Better Place turns out to be too audacious and grandiose to succeed, Agassi's concept may motivate others to launch more-modest efforts that could have more flexibility to adjust to the tech effect.

CHAPTER ELEVEN

Opportunity

Over the years, I spent more time with Scott McNealy than just about any other star of Silicon Valley. McNealy cofounded Sun Microsystems and ran it for two decades, turning it into a computer industry powerhouse. Long before the average person had ever heard of the Internet, McNealy came up with one of the most prescient catchphrases in the history of technology: "The network is the computer." In the 1990s he spoke out against Microsoft's monopolistic tactics when most everyone else was afraid to, often deploying entertaining comic routines, such as referring to Microsoft Windows as the "Microsoft Hairball."

One morning in 2008, we met for breakfast at an unassuming little restaurant in a strip mall tucked into the woods a few minutes' drive from his home. We weren't there to talk about Sun, where he was still chairman but no longer CEO. Instead we discussed one of his more recent passions: applying technology's open-source model to education. Sun was an early proponent of open source, giving the concept a huge boost when it opened up its Java software. (The Java version is a bit of a hybrid, with Sun playing a coaching role in Java's development. But the basic idea has been the same: Lots of programmers from all over the world work on it, and it's free to all.)

By the late 2000s, McNealy had become certain the open-source model could have a gigantic impact on primary school, secondary school, and college education. He funded and helped promote a project called Curriki to create open-source textbooks. Thousands of educators contribute to these online textbooks, which will ultimately be free via the Internet to students and school districts—a development that could undermine traditional textbook publishing the way Wikipedia has undermined encyclopedia publishing. At the restaurant, over his omelet and fruit, McNealy made it clear that the possibilities in open-source education go far beyond textbooks. Before long, McNealy claims, the whole bloated, expensive, lecture-based higher-education system will face the first real challenge to its very existence: open-source, online higher education at a fraction of the cost of four years at Harvard—but good enough for employers who want a college graduate.

"Universities will be forced to decide what they are—you know, are they going to be football teams with libraries attached?" McNealy said. "That's what a lot of them are now."

McNealy talked to me about open-source education for an hour. As the plates were cleared from the table and the waitress refilled our coffee mugs, he leaned forward and, in a quiet voice, said that he hoped education officials actually didn't understand or appreciate the threat. "We don't want the teachers' union fighting this"—at least not before open-source education can gain real momentum.

In fact, by 2008 the idea of some kind of open-source, online, low-cost revolution in education already seemed like a lit fuse, sparking and crackling its way toward an explosion. Here and there, in places ranging from Silicon Valley to Indonesia, a few bold universities and entrepreneurs were taking pokes at the concept. "The economics of traditional schooling are so out of whack that there is an opening for new players," said Fred Fransen, executive director of the Center for Excellence in Higher Education. His organization helps wealthy donors more effectively give their money to universities. From that perch, Fransen sees that the typical university business model looks about as safe from attack as a tower of playing cards in a roomful of two-year-old boys.[1]

The vulnerability sensed by McNealy, Fransen, and others has a lot to do with the fidelity swap. College is a high-fidelity experience. If you want a respected undergraduate degree—the kind that earns you a certain place in the workforce and society—there is pretty much one way to get it. You have to get accepted by an accredited college, pay tuition so costly that it will be one of the most expensive things you buy in your life, and uproot your life and move to a different place—all so you can engage in a rich, all-encompassing experience for four solid years.

Basically, all four-year, professional-grade colleges and universities sit up at the high-fidelity end of education. At the top of the fidelity axis are Harvard, Yale, Stanford—the elite schools. They are fantastically expensive and exclusive, situated on beautiful campuses, each sporting a powerful aura and imparting to its students a valuable identity. Other highly selective universities are grouped together around the high-fidelity end. Public universities are usually a little more convenient (they cost less and let in more applicants), but offer a little less fidelity (not quite the same aura and identity). Still, every option in the bucket of four-year, professional-grade higher education lands high up on the fidelity axis. And, like a lot of things that are very high-fidelity, higher education is very inconvenient. It costs a lot, it's difficult to get in, and you have to move there and live in a tiny dorm with someone you've never met.

But if most of higher education is high-fidelity, is there nothing out at the high-convenience end? Currently there exists no higher-education version of MP3 music files—no way to get a good-enough bachelor's or master's degree that's accepted by professional managers, yet do it in a way that's cheap, easy, and convenient. This is a terrible imbalance. The logic of the fidelity/convenience trade-off is seriously out of balance.

And that's like a giant neon sign announcing, "Monster Opportunity Inside!"

In researching this book, I was struck by the fact that almost every time I explored a market segment through the fidelity-swap lens, there was an obvious set of opposites holding down the high-fidelity and high-convenience positions. There was always a product or experience to love and a product or experience to need. In air travel, you have private jets at one end of the spectrum and Southwest Airlines at the other—both doing well enough. In photography, high-end cameras are balanced by the cameras on cell phones. This seems like a natural state. In any given industry or market, some company or group of competitors vies for the top end of fidelity, while another company or group of competitors vies for the outer edge of convenience. All other players scatter across the fidelity/convenience chart. In everyday business experience, that makes intuitive sense: in a given market, you expect to find successful high-end players, successful low-end players, and a lot of products groping about in between.

Once in a while, a market gets completely out of balance.

Forces conspire to prevent either a high-fidelity or high-convenience player from emerging. All the offerings crowd around one end or the other. Customers, for the most part, accept that this is just the way things are—yet at the same time harbor a feeling that something is wrong. Tension builds. A daring entrepreneur might take a shot at offering an alternative at the empty end of the fidelity/convenience equation, but doesn't quite succeed because forces for the status quo are just too great. But the opening is there, and it's huge. And eventually someone nails it, breaching the levee that had held that market back.

The higher-education market is a lot like that. For centuries the university model dominated because nothing else effectively worked. No technology existed that might deliver an interactive, engaging education experience without gathering students and teachers in the same physical space. In the past century, a powerful social bias set in: only accredited universities were allowed to grant degrees, and most professional jobs required an accredited degree. Even though technology has emerged that might allow for new models of higher education, that neat accreditation ecosystem has locked out innovative competitors. As Ted Leonsis told me, Google could easily rock the higher-education universe by hiring one hundred of the best professors in the world and setting up an Internet-only university funded entirely by advertising—making it free to students. The only problem is that a Google University would have to get accredited by the Higher Learning Commission, which is basically run by and is a part of the traditional higher-education community. In fact, on the commission's website is a warning against interloping competitors: "You should be aware that there is a proliferation of on-line institutions that are either unaccredited or are accredited by agencies that are not recognized by the U.S. Department of Education."[2]

These days, broadband Internet, video games, social networks, and other developments could combine to create an online, inexpensive, super-convenient model for higher education.
You wouldn't get the sights and sounds of a campus, the personal
contact with professors, or beer-soaked frat parties, but you'd
end up with the knowledge you need and the degree to prove it.
The University of Phoenix—which is accredited by the Higher
Learning Commission—is partway there, though it's a hybrid
of online and campus learning. Other organizations, entrepreneurs, and governments are trying to develop super-convenient
universities, often in places outside the United States, including
Hong Kong, Indonesia, and Canada. In McNealy's open-source
vision, perhaps a single, global, open-source university will be
created. McNealy and others are certain that someone, at some
point soon, will open a new kind of university.

The Harvards of the world won't go away. They will continue
to be the high-fidelity players on the fidelity/convenience trade-
off. But a large swath of the population might decide that going
deep into debt before even going to work is too high a price to pay
for a high-fidelity education, when a more convenient version will
do. Just as surely as many consumers left behind long-standing
small-town stores and rushed to Wal-Mart, many students may
decide to put aside a four-year stint at a traditional university for
a cheap, easy, and good-enough degree delivered through laptop
screens and smart phones.

/ / /

When Fred Smith looks back on the 1971 founding of Federal
Express, he wonders if he was a bit nuts. "In retrospect, it was
ridiculous to try to put this system together, which required so

much upfront money, and required changing a lot of government regulations—but I didn't know that at the time," Smith told an interviewer from the Academy of Achievement.[3] Smith graduated from Yale University in 1966 and joined the marines, where he observed the often cacophonous way the military moved supplies. "That's when I sort of crystallized the idea for FedEx," Smith said. Once back on the civilian side, he realized the glaring opportunity. At the time there was only one way to deliver a paper document to someone hundreds or thousands of miles away, and it was far out on the convenience end of the chart. That option was the U.S. Postal Service. It was cheap, ubiquitous, and easy to use. But the postal service was also slow, bureaucratic, and offered little in the way of personal service. If you mailed a legal brief on Monday, you had no idea whether it would get there Wednesday, Thursday, or Friday. The Postal Service dominated mail delivery in the United States for two hundred years for a couple of reasons. First, no one had invented a better way. Second, the U.S. government granted the Postal Service a monopoly on document delivery, which was still in effect when Smith came along.

Smith saw the opening for the first high-fidelity mail service. He would guarantee overnight, door-to-door delivery—for a premium price. He wasn't out to compete against the USPS for everyday mail. Smith saw that the market for *precious* mail was essentially unserved. Emerging technology brought along a way to do it: Smith's service would rely on computers to track packages and manage a complex hub-and-spoke system of trucks and airplanes. But that was only half of Smith's battle. Federal Express launched in 1971 as a package service, but the USPS monopoly on letters didn't end until the late 1970s. By the 1980s, though, businesses wondered how they had lived without FedEx or similar, copycat overnight services for delivering legal documents, important letters, contracts, et cetera. Overnight delivery filled in the empty half of the mail industry's fidelity-swap chart. In just a couple of decades, FedEx became a major company, and kept growing. In 2007 its revenue hit $35 billion.

In the 2000s, India's Tata Motors similarly saw a fidelity/convenience imbalance. One hundred years after Henry Ford democratized the automobile with the Model T, the auto industry had reversed itself and un-democratized the new car. All the major automakers in the 2000s produced cars that cost $15,000 or $20,000 at the low end, and up to tens of thousands more for luxury cars. In part, these highly engineered, feature-rich vehicles were a response to what consumers in wealthy countries wanted—comfort, safety, reliability, and, in many cases, both size and power. The industry's business cycle became self-reinforcing: car companies such as General Motors, Toyota, and Volkswagen built up infrastructures that depended on selling cars for that price. The whole automobile ecosystem relied on selling high-fidelity cars, so that's what the auto companies designed and marketed—in turn helping fuel more demand for high-fidelity cars.

That worked well when most cars were bought by people in relatively rich nations. By the 2000s, though, a different kind of car consumer had emerged in countries such as India, China, Russia, and Brazil. These people started to make enough money to buy cars, but not the high-fidelity cars of the major automakers. The World Bank in 2008 estimated that 800 million people worldwide earned between $3,600 and $11,000 a year. That group, unable to afford a $15,000 car, had been stuck buying rickety used cars or two-wheeled transportation. Hang out in Mumbai or Bangalore in India, for instance, and you'd see families of four zigzagging through chaotic streets while balanced on a scooter like a Cirque du Soleil act.

The result: in the 2000s, the existing auto industry was crowded toward the high-fidelity axis, even as demand soared for a high-convenience car. To most citizens of India, where middle-class incomes were around $6,000 a year, even a Chevy Vibe looked like a high-fidelity, out-of-reach auto. The new-car industry had a gaping hole at the high-convenience end.

Ratan Tata had run his family's 140-year-old company, Tata Group, since 1991. The sprawling conglomerate is often called India's General Electric. Tata Group owned Tata Motors, and Ratan Tata pushed the company to pursue a people's car for the Indian middle class. He dictated that the car must cost one lakh, or 100,000 rupees—which comes to about US $2,500. But it couldn't be as flimsy as an empty beer can on wheels. The one-lakh car had to be a *real* car. In early 2008, Tata unveiled the Nano—an egg-shaped auto that looked like a miniaturized minivan, weighed just 1,322 pounds, and could travel forty-seven miles on a gallon of gas, running at a top speed of sixty-five miles per hour.[4] Before the first car was on the market in mid-2009, analysts figured the Nano would boost the annual number of cars sold in India by 20 percent. Hearing of the Nano, Carlos Ghosn, CEO of the Renault-Nissan alliance, told his companies to develop an under-$3,000 car by 2010; every other major automaker watched the Nano closely. Most people think that high-convenience cars like the Tata are going to be huge.

Of course, the markets for FedEx and the Tata Nano might be obvious in retrospect. But the fidelity/convenience trade-off can help companies see those kinds of opportunities going forward.

One sign to look for in any market: the complete domination by one model, which probably leaves an opening at the other end of the fidelity/convenience trade-off. Internet search might be an example. In the 2000s, search came to be dominated by Google, which is a high-convenience search engine. Google is free, ubiquitous, and easy to get—needed if not always loved. It offers very little fidelity. Google's site is famously bare-bones. It dumps tens of thousands of results onto the user's screen, doing little to figure out what the user is really looking for. Throughout the decade, companies from Ask.com to Cha-Cha to 2008 startup Kosmix (launched by a couple of former Stanford Ph.D.s who allegedly turned down the chance to buy a nascent Google in 1998 for $1 million) have taken shots at creating a higher-fidelity search experience. They all sense an opening on that side of the search business.

There are probably dozens of industries dominated by either fidelity or convenience, leaving a major opportunity at the other end of the market. One such opportunity in the United States is health care.

/ / /

Webster Golinkin didn't come to the health-care field through medical school. He was never remotely a part of the medical establishment. And that probably helped him see the opportunity.

In the 1980s, Golinkin had a sense that most people had no easy way to access information about health. This was before the Internet, in an era when cable television splintered into specialty channels focusing on everything from sports to pets. That gave Golinkin an opening to produce documentaries about health issues—and then evolve that business into a cable channel called

America's Health Network. In 1999, Golinkin sold his company to Fox Entertainment for $135 million; he felt that the blossoming Web would help solve the health information shortage. Yet, as Golinkin told me, while health information became plentiful, millions of people still had no access to decent health care. The people who did have health insurance often found doctor's visits expensive and irritating, especially when they sat for an hour in a fluorescent-lit waiting room before even seeing a nurse. Sensing an opportunity but unsure of how it would play out, Golinkin bought into a nascent company called InterFit, which was doing workplace health screenings for companies such as General Electric. Soon after, InterFit started offering occasional services like flu shots and blood pressure tests at Wal-Mart and other retail stores. "Customers kept telling us they liked our convenience and could we do more," Golinkin said. "That reinforced my view."[5]

The American health-care system had crowded almost entirely into the high-fidelity end of the industry. Health care in the United States was the best in the world, and also the most expensive. There was typically two ways to see a doctor: make an appointment and go to a practice or hospital, or turn up at an emergency room and endure hours of waiting. Fearful of malpractice suits, doctors often overtreated patients with tests and X rays. Insurance companies unwittingly encouraged high fidelity by protecting the insured from the real costs of expensive services. Why not seek high fidelity if insurance is going to cover most of the costs? State regulations, the American Medical Association, and other laws and institutions helped support fidelity and discourage convenience by protecting and certifying the status quo. By the time Golinkin ran InterFit, the hole on the convenience side of health care looked massive and tempting. The big question was the same as that in higher education: Who would crack the code and sweep away the institutional bias?

Golinkin kept thinking about how he could make health care more convenient. One key was to avoid dealing with rare, complex health problems, and instead focus on the routine problems that affect more people more often, and are relatively easy to treat. "We boiled our services down to twenty-five to thirty common conditions and a range of preventive services like basic physicals and immunizations," Golinkin said. "If we could limit the scope of the practice, our system could be much more convenient, efficient, and inexpensive."

Golinkin changed the company's name to RediClinic, got an investment from former AOL CEO Steve Case, and struck deals with Wal-Mart and a couple of other retailers to set up clinics in some of their stores. That way people could get a sore throat checked out, do a little shopping—and have a pharmacy right outside the clinic's doors in case a drug was prescribed. Redi-Clinics tried to take care of every patient in fifteen minutes or less, eliminating frustrating waits. Menus displayed the price of each treatment (pinkeye, $59; cholesterol test, $39). The clinics were staffed by nurse practitioners who could be paid less than doctors. If a medical problem seemed more serious, the nurse practitioners were instructed to recommend that the patient go to a physician. Everything Golinkin did was aimed at creating good-enough health care that was much easier for the mass-market to get. He was driving for convenience—in an industry built around fidelity.

"It was not easy at the beginning," Golinkin said. "The biggest challenge was dealing with the different constituencies that had to be aligned." RediClinic first had to convince retailers that the clinics belonged in their stores, and then had to get consumers to walk in. Insurance companies had to be persuaded to cover visits—otherwise a RediClinic visit would actually cost the consumer more than a visit to a high-fidelity doctor, turning the economics of the fidelity/convenience trade-off upside down. Even after all of that, "we ran into a lot of local physician resistance," Golinkin said. "A lot of them misunderstood what we were doing. They thought we were going to steal their business."

Golinkin wasn't the only one to see this opening. The Walgreens drugstore chain started building in-store clinics in the late 2000s. CVS bought a RediClinic rival, MinuteClinic—which had the motto "You're sick, we're quick."

Still, as of this writing, super-convenience in health care hasn't taken flight.

Golinkin is certain a massive opportunity remains. U.S. citizens spent $2.26 trillion on health care in 2007, almost all of it at the high-fidelity end. The fidelity-swap lens suggests that if someone can figure out convenient health care—a way to handle basic medical needs in a cheaper, more widely available way than traditional doctor's visits—an almost unimaginable amount of money will flow to it.

"The logic of convenient health-care clinics at the end of the day is so compelling, it doesn't make any sense for them not to thrive," Golinkin said. "The toothpaste is out of the tube. This business is here to stay."

CHAPTER TWELVE

Strategy

Last year, I interviewed Ted Leonsis in front of about fifty people at a telecommunications industry lunch. Leonsis owns the Washington Capitals hockey team. He had helped build AOL in the 1990s, invested in a range of startups in the 2000s, and produced documentary films, but he had become famous because of the Caps—which he turned into one of the most exciting teams in the National Hockey League. Leonsis guides his business life by the belief that a successful venture has to be either loved or needed. Pretty much no one was ever going to *need* the Capitals. Leonsis set out to make them loved. By the 2008–9 season, he had assembled a team so dynamic, the Capitals broke franchise records for games that were sold out.

Yet success selling seats has never translated into success on TV for NHL teams. During that live interview, I asked Ted about the National Hockey League's decades-long struggle to get even lukewarm TV ratings. What would he do about it if he could start from scratch? Without hesitation, he said he'd move the league to the Web in a huge way. He'd put every game on line—live, supported by advertising, and free to viewers. Websites such as

Hulu and Joost were finally, in the late 2000s, bringing high-quality television to computer and TV screens via the Internet. It would have been an interesting time for the NHL to take a daring leap into a new medium, attempting to make the NHL the sports league of the digital generation.[1]

A few months later, I visited NHL headquarters in New York. I'd been invited there to learn about the NHL's new digital strategy—which the league clearly was pitching as innovative and forward-thinking. I sat down with Larry Gelfand, the NHL's senior vice president of media sales, and he showed me the overhauled NHL.com website that was due to go live in a couple of weeks.[2] The site was slick and packed with video highlights, but it didn't offer full games, live or recorded. In short, the NHL showed me a well-conceived version of an excellent major-league sports website circa 2008, but it wasn't much more. Excited by Leonsis's vision for a truly bold strategy, I found the NHL's actual strategy disappointing.

The NHL was still relying on TV, even though TV ratings in 2007–8 were down compared with the mid-1990s. Regular season games on nationwide network TV were getting a 1.0 rating—half the audience that watched NHL games on network TV in 1995–96. As discussed earlier, the NHL is not a high-fidelity TV sport. The puck is too small to be easily seen, especially from a distance in a bar. The action and speed are difficult to capture on TV. In addition, in most local U.S. markets, games are carried on cable networks with relatively low production values. On the convenience side, most NHL games air in the United States on obscure cable channels, so games can be hard to find. All in all, the NHL on TV, compared to other major sports, is not great in fidelity or convenience. That leaves the NHL in TV's fidelity belly—unable to get anything but apathy from most of the market.

To implement a winning strategy as a mass-market TV sport, the NHL would have to boost either its fidelity or convenience relative to other TV sports. But it would be tough to beat the NFL on fidelity, and hard to get a lot more convenient unless prime-time network TV started regularly carrying hockey games—which is highly unlikely in the U.S. market. On television, the NHL will have a hard time making much more of an impact.

Here are some other facts the NHL shared with me, from a study done for the league by Experian Consumer Research. Surprisingly, of all the major team sports leagues (NFL, NBA, Major League Baseball), NHL fans have the highest mean household income. They are also younger, more tech-savvy, shop online more, and are 27 percent more likely to own a video game than fans of other leagues. The NHL fan base skews toward young, well-off people comfortable with technology.

One conclusion: a large chunk of NHL fans would welcome being able to see their favorite teams on a laptop screen if they can't see those games on TV. The NHL does offer live games via the Web, but it's a premium service that costs $159 a year—and the price kills the convenience for all but the wealthiest and most devoted fans.

Add it all together, and Ted Leonsis's idea doesn't just sound provocative, it sounds right when viewed through a fidelity-swap lens. For hard-core fans, swinging the live broadcast of games to the Internet for free would give them a high-convenience way to watch their teams and be more connected to the sport. For the broader sports audience, the fidelity/convenience trade-off highlights an interesting opportunity on the Web. As of this writing, none of the major professional or college sports leagues was regularly offering live games for free on the Web. If the NHL were to go to Web broadcasts of games in a big way, the NHL could grab *the* high-fidelity sports position on the Web. The other major sports—football, baseball, basketball, car racing, golf—make too much money on TV to give it up and go to the Web. The NHL is in a uniquely *bad* position on television, which could make it easier to flip over to the Web and become the high-fidelity league associated with the digital generation—much as the NFL became the high-fidelity league for the TV generation.

NHL executives and owners could draw a fidelity-swap chart on a white board, then decide on the buckets that are important to the league and try to figure out where the NHL and its competitors land on the chart. People would probably disagree and debate, but the debate would help the league understand what it really offers different consumers. On any fidelity/convenience chart, in any consumer segment or demographic, if the NHL lands in or near the fidelity belly, then the league should figure out a way to move toward higher convenience or higher fidelity. If that's not possible—as exemplified by the NHL's position in the "TV sports" bucket—the league should stop investing in that bucket, and instead look for a different way to achieve a high-fidelity or high-convenience position. To paraphrase Leonsis, strive to be either loved or needed. And if you can't be either of those, get out.

/ / /

I first worked as an intern at a daily newspaper when I was twenty, and finally left for a magazine just before my forty-seventh birthday. By that time the industry was in serious trouble. Its leaders had apparently run out of ideas for battling Internet-based news and classified advertising, newspaper-company stocks crashed to the floor, and newsrooms big and small cut staff. This gloom came at a time when people were consuming more news than ever before, but not from printed newspapers. Except for notable exceptions like NYTimes.com and WSJ.com, people weren't getting news from newspaper-operated websites, either.

As the tech effect pushed the borders of fidelity and convenience in the production and delivery of news, newspapers didn't keep up. If you were to create a fidelity-swap chart for the professional news business circa 1988, you'd find that newspapers thrived at the time because they offered the most convenient news. For a dime or a quarter, a professionally edited package of news landed on a reader's doorstep in the morning. Readers could look at the paper anytime they wanted—news on demand!—and skip stories or read parts of stories they weren't interested in. No other form of professional news was more comprehensive, easily accessible, and ubiquitous. Even if the local newspaper wasn't loved, it was generally needed by the mass market.

(On the high-fidelity end of professional news in 1988 was CBS's *60 Minutes*. Its brand of in-depth, rich, highly visual news became one of the highest-rated shows on television. It was super-fidelity news. Nobody really needed *60 Minutes*, but the show was loved by a huge audience.)

By 2008, however, an odd thing happened: the tech effect cleaved a generation gap in the consumption of news. A study that year by the Carnegie Corporation found that just 8 percent of people under age thirty-five expected to rely on newspapers for news in the future. The average age of the American newspaper reader was fifty-five.[3] A Pew Survey in the late 2000s found that consumers who were more likely to turn to traditional news outlets, and least likely to rely on the Internet, had a median age of fifty.[4]

So, while mass-market news in 1988 could be represented by

a single fidelity/convenience chart, the market for news in 2008 would have to be broken down into two separate fidelity/convenience charts.

The first chart would be for consumers under the age of forty. In that group, websites serve as the super-convenient news vehicles. Where do newspapers land for the under-forty crowd? Squarely in the fidelity belly, overtaken by technology and considered to be a medium of so-so fidelity and so-so convenience.

The second chart would show the news market for the older generation. For most of those consumers, attitudes toward professional news media haven't changed dramatically in twenty years. They still see newspapers as highly convenient news.

Bottom line, print newspapers have a shot at remaining a high-convenience news brand for people forty and over. But newspapers have absolutely no chance of being anything but an also-ran for consumers under forty.

Which suggests how newspaper companies might invest. The fidelity swap indicates that newspapers should get out of trying to win younger readers to the print product—because it will never work. On the flip side, newspapers continue to hold a strong position in convenience with older readers. It would make sense to cater to them with a print product, and even enhance and exploit that position. Give that audience content it needs, and don't worry if such content further alienates young readers. Print newspapers are destined to lose most of them anyway.

Now, there's an obvious downside in the strategy of appealing only to people who today are over forty years old: that market will inevitably shrink over time. Most newspapers have a website, but many of those websites are still a stepchild to the print product. The fidelity/convenience lens suggests that newspapers should invest in a website that's geared specifically to a younger generation—and is probably nothing at all like the print newspaper.

This split—print for old people; Web for young—would be a radical strategy at any newspaper company. But it's a strategy that newspaper executives might buy into if they look at how their products fit in the trade-off between fidelity and convenience for different audiences.

/ / /

Are you reading this book on paper, or on an electronic reader like the Kindle, or on a laptop screen? Is the very idea of a book changing? Will it survive?

Let's go back to the team that worked on the Kindle for Amazon.com. Few people have spent more effort trying to decide what a book *is*—and why it's been so tough to compete against the printed book with new technology. Interestingly, Amazon came to realize that a book is a high-fidelity experience, even though it's just printed words. As I discussed earlier, the book is such a perfect medium because, when the book's content connects with the reader, the medium of the physical book "disappears"—it gets out of the way and lets the reader become absorbed in the thoughts and words of the author. In that sense, the book is not a physical thing, but a pathway into an author's imagination and world.[5]

To go one step further: a well-written, well-organized book packages the author's brain. It is the purest, richest, most complete way to take what's inside one person's brain and move it into another person's brain. Movies don't do that—films are collaborative efforts, mixing the interpretations of actors, directors, and cameramen with whatever the writer intended. Because of the visual, and aural, nature of film, it's harder for the audience to bring its own imagination as much into play. Articles or columns or blogs are typically too short and focused to carry the reader inside the complexities of another human's thought process. But with a book, you can spend hours inside the author's world. You develop a relationship with the author. As Amazon figured out, nothing is better at transmitting an interesting person's brain. As long as society finds it valuable to consume the stories, research, and thoughts of its intellectual leaders, the basic idea of the book should endure. Paper books will get pressured by electronic versions over time, but the art form should remain vital.

For publishers and authors, though, a critical question centers on the book's position in the broad market for consumers' attention. Here's where channeling the brain of another person—aka the book—runs into trouble. Competition is intense for people's attention, and book reading—or brain-channeling—requires enormous amounts of attention compared with other media such as movies, video games, magazines, websites, live events, and TV shows. The required investment of time to read a book is so high, it makes books extremely inconvenient. That's okay if a book is a very high-fidelity experience. Enough people will give up convenience for fidelity, which is why dedicated music fans flock to concerts despite their great inconvenience. With books, though, the question is whether a given book is high enough in fidelity to make the cost in convenience worthwhile.

That's another way to get at the value proposition of a book— but in the broader context of everything else competing for people's attention. Books can rely on only one strategy to reach a mass audience, and that's to be extremely high-fidelity—in all the ways things become high-fidelity. A bestselling book not only has to be well executed, but it has to attain a social aura that contributes significantly to its readers' identity. Aura and identity often come about when a book rises into the public zeitgeist. Then, reading that book makes you a member of a select club. *The Da Vinci Code* put all those pieces together and sold more than 40 million copies. In the late 2000s, the divorce memoir *Eat, Pray, Love* did, too, and sold 5 million copies.

To people who write, publish, sell, or care about books, the fidelity/convenience trade-off shows this:

• The concept of the book—hundreds of pages, well-organized and well-executed—remains very effective. How it's delivered— paper, Kindle, cell phone—probably doesn't matter as long as the medium can get out of the way and let the reader connect with the author's thoughts and imagination and personality directly.

• To win a sizable audience in the broader market for attention, books have to be very high fidelity to overcome their great inconvenience. That fidelity is a mix of the book's content, its aura, and its ability to add a sense of identity to the person who bought the book.

The good news for publishers and authors is that high-fidelity books still have a place in the mass market. The bad news is that the more technology fractures attention, the more books will seem inconvenient relative to everything else out there. And the more inconvenient books become, the higher they will have to climb up the fidelity axis to make the trade-off worth it for large numbers of people in the mass market.

Publishers and authors have to realize they are in the high-fidelity business. To be successful, books increasingly will have to be high fidelity for at least *some* significant audience—a business-book audience, a cookbook audience, et cetera. The best future roles for publishers and authors, based on the fidelity/convenience trade-off, may be to find, create, and invest in the highest-fidelity books. Books that are only so-so in fidelity perhaps should be left to electronic-only publishers, which can operate at lower cost and charge less for a book. (A lower-cost book would offset at least some of a book's inherent inconvenience.) There could come a time when there will be far fewer book-length works published as paper books.

If you're reading this, you apparently considered my book high enough in fidelity to put up with the inconvenience of taking several hours to tap into the research and experience and stories in my brain. I hope the trade-off was worth it.

Personal Strategy

Jim Collins's *Good to Great*[1] is one of the bestselling hardcover business books of all time. Jim has been a friend since the early 1990s, and as he researched *Good to Great*, I heard about some of the discoveries he was making about the companies that made that good-to-great transition. One conclusion in particular had an effect on me—what he called, in the book, the Hedgehog Concept. It's the notion that great companies figure out what they can do better than anyone else in the world, and then relentlessly focus on that. But the Hedgehog Concept doesn't just apply to companies—it can apply to an individual, too. Jim told me about the concept while he was still writing the book, as the two of us sat in a restaurant in his hometown of Boulder, Colorado, talking about my career. He was pushing me to find my own Hedgehog Concept and stick with it.

Jim also once told me something related, but not a part of his research for the book. He said that there are two ways to get to the top. One is to climb an existing ladder, which can be a bit crowded. The other is to make your own ladder, and put yourself at the top. It's a twist on the Hedgehog Concept—if you can't be the best in an existing category, figure out what you *can* be best at, and create a category that fits. This is what entrepreneurs do when they start their own companies rather than trying to become CEO of IBM or Boeing. It's what Jim did when he left his teaching job at Stanford Business School after coauthoring the national bestseller *Built to Last,* becoming essentially an independent professor of business. Since the profession didn't previously exist, Jim was instantly the best at it.

In the first chapter of this book, I wrote about Daniel Stevens, who runs the Washington, North Carolina, office of the North Carolina Division of Vocational Rehabilitation. Stevens got the office to focus on convenience, telling the local business community that the office could quickly have a good-enough employee at a business's door, ready to work in any emergency.

All of this ties together. Even at the level of the individual, the concepts of the fidelity swap apply. Striving for either high fidelity or high convenience is the best strategy.

Jim Collins's Hedgehog Concept and his ladder concept are all about fidelity. If you're ambitious and willing to be disciplined about your career, you can identify a way to be the high-fidelity player in some fidelity/convenience category. The fidelity trade-off suggests you should figure out what you can do better than anyone else in a particular job category or business, and pursue that.

For example, talented musicians can often play several instruments really well. Let's say a musician loves to play guitar, and can play guitar better than any other instrument she's learned. But since so many people pursue the guitar, she may not have the chops to beat out all of that competition and win a job. Instead of being the high-fidelity guitar player sought by everyone, she'd wind up as a pretty-good-fidelity guitar player who would have a hard time earning a living.

Let's say, though, that she also plays the mandolin, and she's nearly as good at that as guitar. In the reduced universe of mandolin players, she stands a better chance at becoming one of the high-fidelity mandolin players. Although the overall demand for mandolin players isn't as great as that for guitar players, the Hedgehog Concept and the fidelity swap both suggest that she'd be better off trying to be one of the world's best mandolin players than settling for being a less distinguished guitarist. She would be more in demand, and could earn more money, because she would be a high-fidelity mandolin player, rather than a so-so-fidelity guitar player.

In general, the most successful people snag a high-fidelity position on some fidelity/convenience trade-off. Maybe you become the best real estate agent in town, or the best accountant in a firm or the best doctor specializing in a particularly tricky kind of surgery. The higher the fidelity, the more you'll be in demand and the more you can charge for your work—and the less you'll have to be convenient.

Not everyone, of course, is cut out to be the highest-fidelity in *any* bucket. Then the smart strategy is to aim for high convenience. If you can't be the best, most polished real estate agent in town, then be the most convenient. Make yourself available in an instant via text message. Do whatever will make your services easier for a home seller to obtain. Lower your fee—which would add to your convenience—to beat out your competitors. Do everything to be the most convenient.

This was Daniel Stevens's insight in North Carolina. The people he represented were never likely to be high-fidelity employees. But he could make them high-convenience, and that made all the difference.

People who enjoy the most success can be found toward the extremes of fidelity and convenience. People who land in the fidelity belly have the hardest time advancing in their careers. And as with companies, individuals need to be aware of the tech effect. If you're the best or most convenient at a given occupation, technology will inevitably advance and provide the tools for someone to do it better or more conveniently. Like companies, people need to constantly invest, commit, and renew to stay ahead of those around them.

More than 150 years ago, Henry David Thoreau, while working on *Walden* at Walden Pond in Massachusetts, wrote the immortal line "The mass of men lead lives of quiet desperation." But I would argue that's because so many people toil in careers that land inside the fidelity belly.

When you have a clear sense of what distinguishes you from those around you, that sense of quiet desperation disappears.

NOTES

CHAPTER TWO: FIDELITY VERSUS CONVENIENCE

1. Interviews with Jeff Bezos, Amazon.com CEO, New York, April 14–15, 2008.

2. http://www.marxists.org/reference/subject/philosophy/works/ge/benjamin.htm.

3. http://www.engadget.com/2008/03/03/audiophiles-cant-tell-the-difference-between-monster-cable-and/.

4. Interview with Mary Davis, professor, Case Western University, Cleveland, spring 2008.

5. I most recently had this conversation with Ted Leonsis while interviewing him in front of a lunch crowd at a TelecomHUB event in McLean, VA, in May 2008. But I've interviewed Leonsis many times over fifteen years.

6. Pew Research Center, "Things We Can't Live Without: The List Has Grown in the Past Decade" (2006): http://pewsocialtrends.org/pubs/323/luxury-or-necessity.

CHAPTER THREE: THE TRADE-OFF, THE BELLY, AND THE MIRAGE

1. Interview with Irving Wladawsky-Berger, August 2007.

2. Leslie Cauley, "Consumers Ditching Land-line Phones," *USA Today*, May 14, 2008.

3. Deborah Fallows, "Looking for Information about a Place to Live," Pew Internet & American Life Project data memo, December 13, 2006.

4. Pew Research Center, "Things We Can't Live Without: The List Has Grown in the Past Decade" (2006): http://pewsocialtrends.org/pubs/323/luxury-or-necessity.

5. Interview with Bill Gross at Idealab headquarters in Pasadena, CA, February 2008.

CHAPTER FIVE: SUPER-FIDELITY

1. Michael Copeland, "Tesla's Wild Ride," *Fortune*, July 21, 2008.

2. I interviewed Nickel in the summer of 2008 as part of my research for a story on Motorola and the RAZR, which appeared in *Condé Nast Portfolio*, October 2008.

3. Juliann Sivulka, *Stronger Than Dirt: A Cultural History of Advertising Personal Hygiene in America, 1875–1940* (Amherst, NY: Humanity Books, 2001).

4. http://www.foodsafety.gov/~lrd/history2.html.

5. "99 Bottles of Beer on the Wall," *Fortune*, August 18, 2008.

6. "Crocs Sinks on Concern Allure Is Fading as Sales Drop," *Bloomberg*, August 18, 2008.

7. "Steve Wynn's Vegas Vision," *Nightline*, September 26, 2007.

CHAPTER SIX: SUPER-CONVENIENCE

1. Interview with Robert Pittman, New York, November 13, 2007.

2. David A. Hounshell and John K. Smith Jr., *Science and Corporate Strategy: Du Pont R&D, 1902–1980* (New York: Cambridge University Press, 1998).

3. History of Yugo cars, http://www.inet.hr/~bpauric/epov.htm.

4. Kevin Maney, "Webvan Lugs a Dream: Company Hopes Food Will Whet Appetites for Retail Revolution," *USA Today,* June 27, 2000; Harvard Business School case study on Webvan by Andrew McAfee and Mona Ashiya, http://ecommerce.pkeducation.com/blog/wp-content/uploads/2008/03/webvan-sep-2001-hbr.pdf.

5. Sunil Sharma, "Behind the Diffusion Curve: An Analysis of ATM Adoption," paper for the International Monetary Fund, 1991.

6. Michael Barbaro and Steven Greenhouse, "Wal-Mart Chief Writes Off New York," *New York Times,* March 28, 2007.

7. Suzanne Kapner, "Wal-Mart Enters the Ad Age," *Fortune,* August 18, 2008.

8. General Electric ad reproduced at TVHistory.tv: http://www.tvhistory.tv/1939_Dec_Fortune_GE_Advert.JPG.

9. "Number of TV Households in America" chart, http://www.tvhistory.tv/Annual_TV_Households_50-78.JPG.

10. Kevin Maney, "The 3D Dilemma," *Condé Nast Portfolio,* July 2008.

11. Interviews with Bruce Ginsberg, April 2006.

CHAPTER SEVEN: THE WORST PLACE TO BE

1. Interview with Antonio Perez at Dartmouth University, November 2007.

2. Kevin Maney, *Megamedia Shakeout: The Inside Story of the Leaders and the Losers in the Exploding Communications Industry* (New York: John Wiley & Sons, 1995), 244–45.

3. Pew Research Center, *U.S. Daily Newspaper Circulation 1996–2006.*

4. Pew Research Center, *Daily Newspaper Readership by Age Group.*

CHAPTER EIGHT: THE WORST THING TO TRY

1. Howard Schultz and Dori Jones Yang, *Pour Your Heart Into It: How Starbucks Built a Company One Cup at a Time* (New York: Hyperion, 1997), 52.

2. Ibid., 119–20.

3. Interview with Tyler Cowen, economics professor, George Mason University, 2008.

4. Schultz and Yang, *Pour Your Heart Into It*, 307.

5. Michael S. Rosenwald, "Small Coffee Shops Turn the Tables," *Washington Post*, July 14, 2008.

6. Maria Bartiromo, "Howard Schultz on Reinventing Starbucks," *BusinessWeek*, April 9, 2008.

7. David Margolick, "Tall Order," *Condé Nast Portfolio*, July 2008.

8. Melissa Allison, "Starbucks Closing 5 Percent of U.S. Stores," *Seattle Times*, July 2, 2008.

9. Fred Vogelstein, "The Untold Story: How the iPhone Blew Up the Wireless Industry," *Wired*, September 2008.

10. Interview with Marc Andreessen, Palo Alto, CA, September 2008.

11. Andrew Sleigh and Hans von Lewinski, "China: Moving Up the Value Chain," Accenture's *Outlook* Journal, September 2006.

12. Liang Hongfu, "Move Up the Value Chain," *China Daily*, October 18, 2005.

13. Julie Jette, "Selling Luxury to Everyone," *Working Knowledge*, April 18, 2005.

14. http://familyfriendly.wordpress.com/2008/01/21/cruise-passengers-predicted-for-2008-128-million/.

15. Ellen Byron, "To Refurbish Its Image, Tiffany Risks Profits," *Wall Street Journal*, January 10, 2007.

CHAPTER NINE: INNOVATION

1. Interviews with Wladawsky-Berger in August 2007 and April 2008.

2. Kevin Maney, "Vacuum Sweeps into History," *USA Today*, January 15, 2003.

3. Interviews with Colin Angle, 2002 and 2003.

4. Ed Frauenheim, "Robo-Vacuum Wins Wall-to-Wall Praise at Confab," ZDNet, October 21, 2004.

5. Harold Evans, *They Made America* (Boston: Little, Brown & Co., 2004).

6. Scott McCartney, "Airlines Rely on Technology to Manipulate Fare Structure," *Wall Street Journal*, November 3, 1997.

7. Robert G. Cross, *Revenue Management* (New York: Broadway, 1997), 125.

CHAPTER TEN: DISASTERS

1. Interviews with Craig McCaw, November 1994. I still had my notes and files from stories I wrote about Teledesic for *USA Today* back then.

2. I still have the original 1994 packet that Teledesic gave to press and potential investors. One twenty-five-page document lays out the demand for Teledesic; another of equal length describes the system's capabilities.

3. Scott Kirsner, "Breakout Artist," *Wired*, September 2000.

4. John Heilemann, "Reinventing the Wheel," *Time*, December 2, 2001.

5. David Usborne, "Whatever Happened to the Segway?" *The Independent*, May 19, 2007.

6. Kevin Maney, "Keeping in Touch: Apple Puts Computer in Your Pocket," *USA Today*, August 3, 1993.

7. Kevin Maney, "A PDA for the Holidays? Qxfzg!" *USA Today*, December 16, 1993.

8. This section comes from personal interviews with Jeff Hawkins and Donna Dubinsky about Palm's early days, in March 2006.

9. Daniel Roth, "Driven: Shai Agassi's Audacious Plan to Put Electric Cars on the Road," *Wired*, August 18, 2008.

10. From the Web 2.0 Summit in San Francisco, October 2008. Agassi was interviewed by cohost Tim O'Reilly.

CHAPTER ELEVEN: OPPORTUNITY

1. Interview with Fred Fransen, Center for Excellence in Higher Education, March 2008.

2. http://www.ncahlc.org/index.php?option=com_content&task=view&id=80&Itemid=108.

3. http://www.achievement.org/autodoc/page/smioint-1.

4. Scott Carney, "The $3,000, 33-Horsepower, Snap-Together Ride to the Future," *Wired*, July 2008.

5. Interview with Web Golinkin, November 2008.

CHAPTER 12. STRATEGY

1. Interviews with Ted Leonsis, 2008.

2. Visit to National Hockey League headquarters, October 2008.

3. Eric Alterman, "Out of Print," *The New Yorker*, March 31, 2008.

4. "The State of the Media 2008," Pew Research Center's Project for Excellence in Journalism.

5. Interview with Jeff Bezos, April 2008.

CHAPTER TWELVE POINT FIVE: PERSONAL STRATEGY

1. Jim Collins, *Good to Great* (New York: HarperCollins, 2001).

INDEX

ABOUT THE AUTHOR

Kevin Maney, the author of *Megamedia Shakeout* and *The Maverick and His Machine,* is a contributor to *Fortune, The Atlantic,* and *Fast Company* and was a contributing editor at *Condé Nast Portfolio.* He often appears on NPR, ABC News NOW, CNBC, and many other TV and radio outlets. Maney wrote a technology column for *USA Today* for almost two decades. He lives outside of Washington, D.C.